Keto Diet

Cookbook for Beginners 2024

1800 Days of Low Carb Keto Diet Recipes for Easy Weight Loss and Eating Well Every Day Includes Stress-Free 28-Day Meal Plan

Cheryl K. Martin

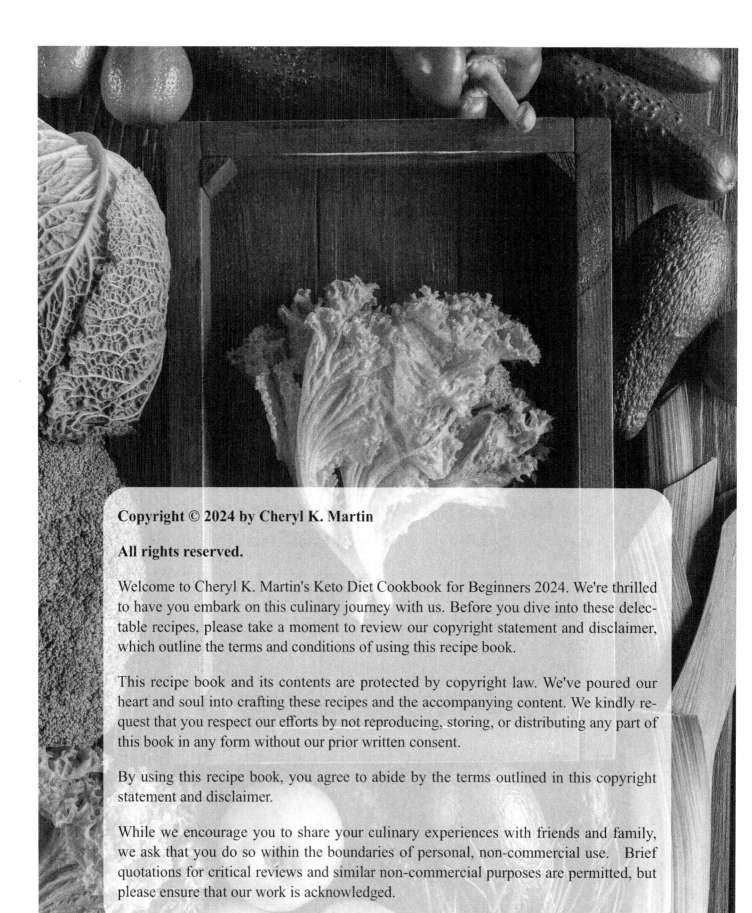

CONTENTS

Soups, Stew & Salads Recipes   33

Pork, Beef & Lamb Recipes   42

Poultry Recipes   52

Desserts And Drinks Recipes

Shopping List

Appendix A: Measurement Conversions

Appendix B: Recipes Index

INTRODUCTION

Cheryl K. Martin is a prominent figure in the realm of ketogenic living, a dedicated health advocate, and a culinary enthusiast whose passion for nutritious, low-carb cuisine has transformed countless lives. Cheryl's professional journey began in the field of nutrition and dietetics, where she honed her expertise in understanding the intricacies of food and its impact on the human body. Her background in this field not only equipped her with the knowledge needed to navigate the complex world of diets and nutrition but also instilled in her a genuine desire to make a positive difference in people's lives through food.

Cheryl spent years meticulously researching and experimenting with ketogenic principles to develop a profound understanding of how the diet works and its potential benefits. As she embarked on the writing process, Cheryl delved deep into the science behind ketosis, metabolic adaptation, and the intricate interplay of macronutrients that make the ketogenic diet a powerful tool for weight management, improved mental clarity, and overall well-being. This comprehensive understanding formed the foundation upon which "The Keto Diet Cookbook" was built.

Cheryl's commitment to making keto accessible and enjoyable for all shines through in every aspect of her cookbook. She crafted each recipe with precision, focusing not only on nutritional accuracy but also on delivering a delightful culinary experience. Her recipes encompass a wide range of flavors and textures, ensuring that there is something for everyone, whether they are keto novices or seasoned enthusiasts.

Beyond the recipes, Cheryl's dedication to her readers' success is evident in the practical advice, tips, and meal-planning strategies woven throughout the book. Her warm and relatable writing style creates a supportive and inviting atmosphere, guiding readers on their journey to healthier living with encouragement and expertise.

Cheryl K. Martin's "The Keto Diet Cookbook" is more than just a cookbook; it is a testament to her passion for health, nutrition, and the art of cooking. With her guidance and expertise, Cheryl empowers individuals to embrace the ketogenic lifestyle as a sustainable and delicious path towards better health and vitality. Her commitment to wellness, coupled with her culinary prowess, ensures that "The Keto Diet Cookbook" is not just a collection of recipes but a comprehensive guide that can transform lives, one wholesome and flavorful dish at a time.

What is ketosis?

Ketosis is a process that occurs when your body uses fat as its main fuel source. Normally, your body uses blood sugar (glucose) as its key energy source.

You typically get glucose in your diet by eating carbohydrates (carbs) such as starches and sugars. Your body breaks the carbohydrates down into glucose and then uses the glucose as fuel. Your liver stores the rest and releases it as needed.

When your carb intake is very low, these glucose stores drain down. Since your body doesn't have enough carbs to burn for energy, it burns fat instead. As your body breaks down fat, it produces a compound called ketones. The ketones, or ketone bodies, become your body and brain's main source of energy.

The fat your body uses to create ketones may come from your diet (nutritional ketosis), or it may come from your body's fat stores. Your liver produces a small amount of ketones on its own. But when your glucose level decreases, your insulin level decreases. This causes your liver to ramp up the production of ketones to ensure it can provide enough energy for your brain. Therefore, your blood has high levels of ketones during ketosis.

What is the Ketosis Diet?

The ketogenic (keto) diet changes the way your body uses food. Typically, carbohydrates in your diet provide most of the fuel your body needs. The keto diet reduces the number of carbs you eat and teaches your body to burn fat for fuel instead.

The keto diet is high in fat, moderate in protein and low in carbohydrates. The standard keto diet consists of 70% to 80% fats, 10% to 20% proteins and 5% to 10% carbohydrates.

Many nutrient-rich foods contain high amounts of carbohydrates. This includes whole grains, fruits and vegetables. Carbs from all sources are restricted on the keto diet. So you'll have to cut out all bread, cereal and other grains and make serious cuts to your fruit and vegetable intake. The types of foods that provide fat for the keto diet include:

- Meats and fish.

- Eggs.

- Nuts and seeds.

- Butter and cream.

- Cheese.

- Oils such as olive oil and canola oil.

A List of Acceptable Foods for the Standard Ketogenic Diet

Nonstarchy vegetables like leafy greens, broccoli, cauliflower, cabbage, peppers, mushrooms, onions, and rhubarb

Dairy, including eggs and cheese

Protein like beef, pork, poultry, fish, shellfish, and soybeans

Nuts and seeds, including walnuts, almonds, pistachios, sunflower seeds, and pumpkin seeds

Fats like plant-based oils and butter

Fruits like avocado, berries (in moderation), and tomatoes

Foods You Should Avoid or Limit on the Ketogenic Diet

Processed foods like crackers, corn chips, and potato chips

Sweets, including candy, cookies, brownies, and cake

Grains of all kinds, including bread, pasta, rice, and quinoa

High-carb fruits like melons and tropical fruits

Keto Diet

Benefits of the Keto Diet

At least in the short term, studies show that keto diets get amazing and quick results for weight loss. They can also improve conditions like type 2 diabetes.

These benefits come from many factors, including:

1. **Lower insulin levels.** When you eat foods with carbohydrates and to a lesser extent protein, you raise your blood sugar levels. Insulin steps in to lower those blood sugar levels, delivering glucose to your cells for energy or to store for backup fuel called glycogen. But high insulin levels — which can happen when you eat too many carbohydrates — can prevent fat loss. On a keto diet, you keep insulin levels lower. Low insulin means that your body can more easily access fat stores for fuel.

2. **Hormonal balance.** Keto diets help balance other hormones besides insulin. Among those hunger-regulating hormones is leptin, a hormone that tells your brain to stop eating. Ghrelin has the opposite effect: This hormone tells you to eat more. When these and other hormones stay in balance on a keto diet, you're less likely to have hunger and cravings.

3. **Lower inflammation levels.** Chronic inflammation plays a role in obesity but also diseases including diabetes. Sugar, in all its many disguises, is an inflammatory food. On a keto diet, you keep your sugar and overall carbohydrate intake very low. When you combine that approach with whole, unprocessed foods, you lower inflammation levels.

These and other advantages of a keto diet help you lose weight and reduces your risk of disease. People on keto diets also report more energy, focus, and mental clarity.

28 Day Meal Plan

DAY	BREAKFAST	LUNCH	DINNER
1	Walnut Cookies 81	Sausage Roll 24	Stir Fried Broccoli 'n Chicken 53
2	Green And Fruity Smoothie 81	Walnuts With Tofu 24	Quattro Formaggi Chicken 53
3	Chocolate Chip Cookies 81	Grilled Spicy Eggplant 24	Rosemary Grilled Chicken 54
4	Lettuce Green Shake 81	Keto Cauliflower Hash Browns 25	Chicken In Creamy Tomato Sauce 54
5	Berry Tart 82	Cremini Mushroom Stroganoff 25	Creamy Stuffed Chicken With Parma Ham 53
6	Strawberry Yogurt Shake 82	Garlic Lemon Mushrooms 25	Cheddar Chicken Tenders 54
7	Nutty Arugula Yogurt Smoothie 82	Greek Styled Veggie-rice 26	Zucchini Spaghetti With Turkey Bolognese Sauce 54
8	Five Greens Smoothie 83	Pumpkin Bake 25	Basil Turkey Meatballs 55
9	Strawberry-coconut Shake 83	Grilled Cheese The Keto Way 26	Chicken Skewers With Celery Fries 55
10	Passion Fruit Cheesecake Slices 83	Portobello Mushroom Burgers 26	Chicken With Green Sauce 55
11	Green Tea Brownies With Macadamia Nuts 84	Cauliflower & Mushrooms Stuffed Peppers 27	Turkey & Mushroom Bake 56
12	Granny Smith Apple Tart 84	Creamy Artichoke And Spinach 28	Stewed Chicken Salsa 55
13	Mixed Berry Nuts Mascarpone Bowl 84	Bell Pepper & Pumpkin With Avocado Sauce 28	Turkey, Coconut And Kale Chili 57
14	Vanilla Chocolate Mousse 85	Cilantro-lime Guacamole 27	Grilled Chicken Wings 56

DAY	BREAKFAST	LUNCH	DINNER
15	Strawberry-choco Shake 84	Greek-style Zucchini Pasta 28	Turkey & Leek Soup 56
16	Creamy Choco Shake 85	Herb Butter With Parsley 28	One-pot Chicken With Mushrooms And Spinach 57
17	Cinnamon And Turmeric Latte 85	Onion & Nuts Stuffed Mushrooms 29	Chicken And Spinach Stir Fry 58
18	Coconut Cheesecake 85	Cream Of Zucchini And Avocado 29	Chicken Country Style 56
19	Nutritiously Green Milk Shake 86	:Mushroom & Cauliflower Bake 29	Chicken And Spinach 58
20	Blackberry-chocolate Shake 86	Paprika 'n Cajun Seasoned Onion Rings 30	Chicken Stew With Sun-dried Tomatoes 57
21	Smarties Cookies 87	Cauliflower Risotto With Mushrooms 29	Sweet Garlic Chicken Skewers 58
22	Baby Kale And Yogurt Smoothie 87	Stuffed Cremini Mushrooms 30	Cheesy Chicken Bake With Zucchini 59
23	Lemon Cheesecake Mousse 87	Walnut Tofu Sauté 31	Slow Cooked Chicken Drumstick 59
24	Onion Cheese Muffins 16	Bell Pepper Stuffed Avocado 31	Grilled Paprika Chicken With Steamed Broccoli 59
25	Spicy Devilled Eggs With Herbs 16	Wild Mushroom And Asparagus Stew 30	Easy Chicken Vindaloo 60
26	Parsnip And Carrot Fries With Aioli 17	Keto Pizza Margherita 31	Turkey Enchilada Bowl 60
27	Devilled Eggs With Sriracha Mayo 17	Garlic And Greens 31	Sticky Cranberry Chicken Wings 69
28	Sour Cream And Carrot Sticks 17	Coconut Cauliflower & Parsnip Soup 32	Chicken With Monterey Jack Cheese 60

Appetizers, Snacks & Side Dishes Recipes

Appetizers, Snacks & Side Dishes Recipes

Apricot And Soy Nut Trail Mix

Servings: 20
Cooking Time: 10 Minutes

Ingredients:
- ¼ cup dried apricots, chopped
- 1 cup pumpkin seeds
- ½ cup roasted cashew nuts
- 1 cup roasted, shelled pistachios
- Salt to taste
- 3 tbsp MCT oil or coconut oil

Directions:
1. In a medium mixing bowl, place all ingredients.
2. Thoroughly combine.
3. Bake in the oven for 10 minutes at 3750F.
4. In 20 small zip-top bags, get ¼ cup of the mixture and place in each bag.
5. One zip-top bag is equal to one serving.
6. If properly stored, this can last up to two weeks.

Nutrition Info:
- Per Servings 4.6g Carbs, 5.2g Protein, 10.75g Fat, 129 Calories

Crab Stuffed Mushrooms

Servings: 3
Cooking Time: 25 Minutes

Ingredients:
- 2 tbsp minced green onion
- 1 cup cooked crabmeat, chopped finely
- ¼ cup Monterey Jack cheese, shredded
- 1 tsp lemon juice
- ¼ lb, fresh button mushrooms
- Pepper and salt to taste
- 3 tablespoons olive oil

Directions:
1. Destem mushrooms, wash, and drain well.
2. Chop mushroom stems.
3. Preheat oven to 400oF and lightly grease a baking pan with cooking spray.
4. In a small bowl, whisk well green onion, crabmeat, lemon juice, dill, and chopped mushroom stems.
5. Evenly spread mushrooms on prepared pan with cap sides up. Evenly spoon crabmeat mixture on top of mushroom caps.
6. Pop in the oven and bake for 20 minutes.
7. Remove from oven and sprinkle cheese on top.

8. Return to oven and broil for 3 minutes.
9. Serve and enjoy.

Nutrition Info:
- Per Servings 10g Carbs, 7.9g Protein, 17.3g Fat, 286 Calories

Air Fryer Garlic Chicken Wings

Servings: 4
Cooking Time: 25 Minutes

Ingredients:
- 16 pieces chicken wings
- ¾ cup almond flour
- 4 tablespoons minced garlic
- ¼ cup butter, melted
- 2 tablespoons Stevia powder
- Salt and pepper to taste

Directions:
1. Preheat oven to 400oF.
2. In a mixing bowl, combine the chicken wings, almond flour, Stevia powder, and garlic. Season with salt and pepper to taste.
3. Place in a lightly greased cookie sheet in an even layer and cook for 25 minutes.
4. Halfway through the cooking time, turnover chicken.
5. Once cooked, place in a bowl and drizzle with melted butter. Toss to coat.
6. Serve and enjoy.

Nutrition Info:
- Per Servings 7.8g Carbs, 23.7g Protein, 26.9g Fat, 365 Calories

Cheesy Chicken Fritters With Dill Dip

Servings: 4
Cooking Time: 40 Minutes + Cooling Time

Ingredients:
- 1 lb chicken breasts, thinly sliced
- 1 ¼ cup mayonnaise
- ¼ cup coconut flour
- 2 eggs
- Salt and black pepper to taste
- 1 cup grated mozzarella cheese
- 4 tbsp chopped dill
- 3 tbsp olive oil
- 1 cup sour cream
- 1 tsp garlic powder

- 1 tbsp chopped parsley
- 2 tbsp finely chopped onion

Directions:

1. In a bowl, mix 1 cup of the mayonnaise, 3 tbsp of dill, sour cream, garlic powder, onion, and salt. Cover the bowl with plastic wrap and refrigerate for 30 minutes.

2. Mix the chicken, remaining mayonnaise, coconut flour, eggs, salt, pepper, mozzarella, and remaining dill, in a bowl. Cover the bowl with plastic wrap and refrigerate it for 2 hours. After the marinating time is over, remove from the fridge.

3. Place a skillet over medium fire and heat the olive oil. Fetch 2 tablespoons of chicken mixture into the skillet, use the back of a spatula to flatten the top. Cook for 4 minutes, flip, and fry for 4 more.

4. Remove onto a wire rack and repeat the cooking process until the batter is finished, adding more oil as needed. Garnish the fritters with parsley and serve with dill dip.

Nutrition Info:

- Per Servings 0.8g Carbs, 12g Protein, 7g Fat, 151 Calories

Onion Cheese Muffins

Servings: 6
Cooking Time: 20 Minutes

Ingredients:

- ¼ cup Colby jack cheese, shredded
- ¼ cup shallots, minced
- 1 cup almond flour
- 1 egg
- 3 tbsp sour cream
- ½ tsp salt
- 3 tbsp melted butter or oil

Directions:

1. Line 6 muffin tins with 6 muffin liners. Set aside and preheat oven to 350oF.

2. In a bowl, stir the dry and wet ingredients alternately. Mix well using a spatula until the consistency of the mixture becomes even.

3. Scoop a spoonful of the batter to the prepared muffin tins.

4. Bake for 20 minutes in the oven until golden brown.

5. Serve and enjoy.

Nutrition Info:

- Per Servings 4.6g Carbs, 6.3g Protein, 17.4g Fat, 193 Calories

Spicy Devilled Eggs With Herbs

Servings: 4
Cooking Time: 30 Minutes

Ingredients:

- 12 large eggs
- 1 ½ cups water
- 6 tbsp mayonnaise
- Salt and chili pepper to taste
- 1 tsp mixed dried herbs
- ½ tsp sugar-free Worcestershire sauce
- ¼ tsp Dijon mustard
- A pinch of sweet paprika
- Chopped parsley to garnish
- Ice water Bath

Directions:

1. Pour the water into a saucepan, add the eggs, and bring to boil on high heat for 10 minutes. Cut the eggs in half lengthways and remove the yolks into a medium bowl. Use a fork to crush the yolks.

2. Add the mayonnaise, salt, chili pepper, dried herbs, Worcestershire sauce, mustard, and paprika. Mix together until a smooth paste has formed. Then, spoon the mixture into the piping bag and fill the egg white holes with it. Garnish with the chopped parsley and serve immediately.

Nutrition Info:

- Per Servings 0.4g Carbs, 6.7g Protein, 9.3g Fat, 112 Calories

Cajun Spiced Pecans

Servings: 10
Cooking Time: 10 Minutes

Ingredients:

- 1-pound pecan halves
- ¼ cup butter
- 1 packet Cajun seasoning mix
- ¼ teaspoon ground cayenne pepper
- Salt and pepper to taste

Directions:

1. Place a nonstick saucepan on medium fire and melt butter.

2. Add pecans and remaining ingredients.

3. Sauté for 5 minutes.

4. Remove from fire and let it cool completely.

5. Serve and enjoy.

Nutrition Info:

- Per Servings 6.8g Carbs, 4.2g Protein, 37.3g Fat, 356.5 Calories

Parsnip And Carrot Fries With Aioli

Servings: 4
Cooking Time: 40 Minutes

Ingredients:
- 4 tbsp mayonnaise
- 2 garlic cloves, minced
- Salt and black pepper to taste
- 3 tbsp lemon juice
- Parsnip and Carrots Fries:
- 6 medium parsnips, julienned
- 3 large carrots, julienned
- 2 tbsp olive oil
- 5 tbsp chopped parsley
- Salt and black pepper to taste

Directions:
1. Preheat the oven to 400ºF. Make the aioli by mixing the mayonnaise with garlic, salt, pepper, and lemon juice; then refrigerate for 30 minutes.
2. Spread the parsnip and carrots on a baking sheet. Drizzle with olive oil, sprinkle with salt, and pepper, and rub the seasoning into the veggies. Bake for 35 minutes. Remove and transfer to a plate. Garnish the vegetables with parsley and serve with the chilled aioli.

Nutrition Info:
- Per Servings 4.4g Carbs, 2.1g Protein, 4.1g Fat, 205 Calories

Devilled Eggs With Sriracha Mayo

Servings: 4
Cooking Time: 15 Minutes

Ingredients:
- 8 large eggs
- 3 cups water
- Ice water bath
- 3 tbsp sriracha sauce
- 4 tbsp mayonnaise
- Salt to taste
- ¼ tsp smoked paprika

Directions:
1. Bring eggs to boil in salted water in a pot over high heat, and then reduce the heat to simmer for 10 minutes. Transfer eggs to an ice water bath, let cool completely and peel the shells.
2. Slice the eggs in half height wise and empty the yolks into a bowl. Smash with a fork and mix in sriracha sauce, mayonnaise, and half of the paprika until smooth.
3. Spoon filling into a piping bag with a round nozzle and fill the egg whites to be slightly above the brim. Garnish with remaining paprika and serve immediately.

Nutrition Info:
- Per Servings 1g Carbs, 4g Protein, 19g Fat, 195 Calories

Sour Cream And Carrot Sticks

Servings: 3
Cooking Time: 0 Minutes

Ingredients:
- 1 sweet onion, peeled and minced
- ½ cup sour cream
- 2 tbsp mayonnaise
- 4 tablespoons olive oil
- 4 stalks celery, cut into 3-inch lengths
- Pepper and salt to taste

Directions:
1. In a bowl, whisk well sour cream and mayonnaise until thoroughly combined.
2. Stir in onion and mix well.
3. Let it sit for an hour in the fridge and serve with celery sticks on the side.

Nutrition Info:
- Per Servings 7g Carbs, 3g Protein, 13g Fat, 143 Calories

Roasted Stuffed Piquillo Peppers

Servings: 8
Cooking Time: 20 Minutes

Ingredients:
- 8 canned roasted piquillo peppers
- 1 tbsp olive oil
- 3 slices prosciutto, cut into thin slices
- 1 tbsp balsamic vinegar
- Filling:
- 8 ounces goat cheese
- 3 tbsp heavy cream
- 3 tbsp chopped parsley
- ½ tsp minced garlic
- 1 tbsp olive oil
- 1 tbsp chopped mint

Directions:
1. Mix all filling ingredients in a bowl. Place in a freezer bag, press down and squeeze, and cut off the bottom. Drain and deseed the peppers. Squeeze about 2 tbsp of the filling into each pepper.
2. Wrap a prosciutto slice onto each pepper. Secure with toothpicks. Arrange them on a serving platter. Sprinkle the olive oil and vinegar over.

Nutrition Info:
- Per Servings 2.5g Carbs, 6g Protein, 11g Fat, 132 Calories

Squid Salad With Mint, Cucumber & Chili Dressing

Servings: 4
Cooking Time: 30 Minutes

Ingredients:
- 4 medium squid tubes, cut into strips
- ½ cup mint leaves
- 2 medium cucumbers, halved and cut in strips
- ½ cup coriander leaves, reserve the stems
- ½ red onion, finely sliced
- Salt and black pepper to taste
- 1 tsp fish sauce
- 1 red chili, roughly chopped
- 1 tsp swerve
- 1 clove garlic
- 2 limes, juiced
- 1 tbsp chopped coriander
- 1tsp olive oil

Directions:
1. In a salad bowl, mix mint leaves, cucumber strips, coriander leaves, and red onion. Season with salt, pepper and a little drizzle of olive oil; set aside. In the mortar, pound the coriander stems, red chili, and swerve into a paste using the pestle. Add the fish sauce and lime juice, and mix with the pestle.
2. Heat a skillet over high heat on a stovetop and sear the squid on both sides to lightly brown, about 5 minutes. Pour the squid on the salad and drizzle with the chili dressing. Toss the ingredients with two spoons, garnish with coriander, and serve the salad as a single dish or with some more seafood.

Nutrition Info:
- Per Servings 2.1g Carbs, 24.6g Protein, 22.5g Fat, 318 Calories

Spiced Gruyere Crisps

Servings: 4
Cooking Time: 10 Minutes

Ingredients:
- 2 cups gruyere cheese, shredded
- ½ tsp garlic powder
- ¼ tsp onion powder
- 1 rosemary sprig, minced
- ½ tsp chili powder

Directions:
1. Set oven to 400ºF. Coat two baking sheets with parchment paper.
2. Mix Gruyere cheese with the seasonings. Take 1 tablespoon of cheese mixture and form small mounds on the baking sheets. Bake for 6 minutes. Leave to cool. Serve.

Nutrition Info:
- Per Servings 2.9g Carbs, 14.5g Protein, 15g Fat, 205 Calories

Buttery Herb Roasted Radishes

Servings: 6
Cooking Time: 25 Minutes

Ingredients:
- 2 lb small radishes, greens removed
- 3 tbsp olive oil
- Salt and black pepper to season
- 3 tbsp unsalted butter
- 1 tbsp chopped parsley
- 1 tbsp chopped tarragon

Directions:
1. Preheat oven to 400ºF and line a baking sheet with parchment paper. Toss radishes with oil, salt, and black pepper. Spread on baking sheet and roast for 20 minutes until browned.
2. Heat butter in a large skillet over medium heat to brown and attain a nutty aroma, 2 to 3 minutes.
3. Take out the parsnips from the oven and transfer to a serving plate. Pour over the browned butter atop and sprinkle with parsley and tarragon. Serve with roasted rosemary chicken.

Nutrition Info:
- Per Servings 2g Carbs, 5g Protein, 14g Fat, 160 Calories

Easy Garlic Keto Bread

Servings: 1
Cooking Time: 1 Minute 30 Seconds

Ingredients:
- 1 large egg
- 1 tbsp milk
- 1 tbsp coconut flour
- 1 tbsp almond flour
- ¼ tsp baking powder
- Salt to taste

Directions:
1. Mix all ingredients in a bowl until well combined.
2. Pour into a mug and place in the microwave oven.
3. Cook for 1 minute and 30 seconds.
4. Once cooked, invert the mug.
5. Allow to cool before slicing.

Nutrition Info:
- Per Servings 3g Carbs, 4g Protein, 7g Fat, 75 Calories

Buttered Broccoli

Servings: 6
Cooking Time: 10 Minutes

Ingredients:
- 1 broccoli head, florets only
- Salt and black pepper to taste
- ¼ cup butter

Directions:
1. Place the broccoli in a pot filled with salted water and bring to a boil. Cook for about 3 minutes.
2. Melt the butter in a microwave. Drain the broccoli and transfer to a plate. Drizzle the butter over and season with some salt and pepper.

Nutrition Info:
- Per Servings 5.5g Carbs, 3.9g Protein, 7.8g Fat, 114 Calories

Cardamom And Cinnamon Fat Bombs

Servings: 10
Cooking Time: 3 Minutes

Ingredients:
- ¼ tsp ground cardamom (green)
- ¼ tsp ground cinnamon
- ½ cup unsweetened shredded coconut
- ½ tsp vanilla extract
- 3-oz unsalted butter, room temperature

Directions:
1. Place a nonstick pan on medium fire and toast coconut until lightly browned.
2. In a bowl, mix all ingredients.
3. Evenly roll into 10 equal balls.
4. Let it cool in the fridge.
5. Serve and enjoy.

Nutrition Info:
- Per Servings 0.4g Carbs, 0.4g Protein, 10.0g Fat, 90 Calories

Turkey Pastrami & Mascarpone Cheese Pinwheels

Servings: 4
Cooking Time: 40 Minutes

Ingredients:
- Cooking spray
- 8 oz mascarpone cheese
- 10 oz turkey pastrami, sliced
- 10 canned pepperoncini peppers, sliced and drained

Directions:
1. Lay a 12 x 12 plastic wrap on a flat surface and arrange the pastrami all over slightly overlapping each other. Spread the cheese on top of the salami layers and arrange the pepperoncini on top.
2. Hold two opposite ends of the plastic wrap and roll the pastrami. Twist both ends to tighten and refrigerate for 2 hours. Unwrap the salami roll and slice into 2-inch pinwheels. Serve.

Nutrition Info:
- Per Servings 0g Carbs, 13g Protein, 24g Fat, 266 Calories

Curry ' N Poppy Devilled Eggs

Servings: 6
Cooking Time: 8 Minutes

Ingredients:
- ½ cup mayonnaise
- ½ tbsp poppy seeds
- 1 tbsp red curry paste
- 6 eggs
- ¼ tsp salt

Directions:
1. Place eggs in a small pot and add enough water to cover it. Bring to a boil without a cover, lower fire to a simmer and simmer for 8 minutes.
2. Immediately dunk in ice-cold water once done the cooking. Peel eggshells and slice eggs in half lengthwise.
3. Remove yolks and place them in a medium bowl. Add the rest of the ingredients in the bowl except for the egg whites. Mix well.
4. Evenly return the yolk mixture into the middle of the egg whites.
5. Serve and enjoy.

Nutrition Info:
- Per Servings 1.0g Carbs, 6.0g Protein, 19.0g Fat, 200 Calories

Party Bacon And Pistachio Balls

Servings: 8
Cooking Time: 45 Minutes

Ingredients:
- 8 bacon slices, cooked and chopped
- 8 ounces Liverwurst
- ¼ cup chopped pistachios
- 1 tsp Dijon mustard
- 6 ounces cream cheese

Directions:
1. Combine the liverwurst and pistachios in the bowl of your food processor. Pulse until smooth. Whisk the cream cheese and mustard in another bowl. Make 12 balls out of the liverwurst mixture.
2. Make a thin cream cheese layer over. Coat with bacon, arrange on a plate and chill for 30 minutes.

Nutrition Info:
• Per Servings 1.5g Carbs, 7g Protein, 12g Fat, 145 Calories

Cheddar Cheese Chips

Servings: 4
Cooking Time: 8 Minutes

Ingredients:
• 8 oz cheddar cheese or provolone cheese or Edam cheese, in slices
• ½ tsp paprika powder

Directions:
1. Line baking sheet with foil and preheat oven to 400F.
2. Place cheese slices on a baking sheet and sprinkle the paprika powder on top.
3. Pop in the oven and bake for 8 to 10 minutes.
4. Pay an attention when the timer reaches 6 to 7 minutes as a burnt cheese tastes bitter.
5. Serve and enjoy.

Nutrition Info:
• Per Servings 2.0g Carbs, 13.0g Protein, 19.0g Fat, 228 Calories

Cheesy Green Bean Crisps

Servings: 6
Cooking Time: 30 Minutes

Ingredients:
• Cooking spray
• ¼ cup shredded pecorino romano cheese
• ¼ cup pork rind crumbs
• 1 tsp garlic powder
• Salt and black pepper to taste
• 2 eggs
• 1 lb green beans, thread removed

Directions:
1. Preheat oven to 425ºF and line two baking sheets with foil. Grease with cooking spray and set aside.
2. Mix the pecorino, pork rinds, garlic powder, salt, and black pepper in a bowl. Beat the eggs in another bowl. Coat green beans in eggs, then cheese mixture and arrange evenly on the baking sheets.
3. Grease lightly with cooking spray and bake for 15 minutes to be crispy. Transfer to a wire rack to cool before serving. Serve with sugar-free tomato dip.

Nutrition Info:
• Per Servings 3g Carbs, 5g Protein, 19g Fat, 210 Calories

Spinach And Ricotta Gnocchi

Servings: 4
Cooking Time: 13 Minutes

Ingredients:
• 3 cups chopped spinach
• 1 cup ricotta cheese
• 1 cup Parmesan cheese , grated
• ¼ tsp nutmeg powder
• 1 egg, cracked into a bowl
• Salt and black pepper
• Almond flour, on standby
• 2 ½ cups water
• 2 tbsp butter

Directions:
1. To a bowl, add the ricotta cheese, half of the parmesan cheese, egg, nutmeg powder, salt, spinach, almond flour, and pepper. Mix well. Make quenelles of the mixture using 2 tbsp and set aside.
2. Bring the water to boil over high heat on a stovetop, about 5 minutes. Place one gnocchi onto the water, if it breaks apart; add some more flour to the other gnocchi to firm it up.
3. Put the remaining gnocchi in the water to poach and rise to the top, about 2 minutes. Remove the gnocchi with a perforated spoon to a serving plate.
4. Melt the butter in a microwave and pour over the gnocchi. Sprinkle with the remaining parmesan cheese and serve with a green salad.

Nutrition Info:
• Per Servings 4.1g Carbs, 6.5g Protein, 8.3g Fat, 125 Calories

Baba Ganoush Eggplant Dip

Servings: 4
Cooking Time: 80 Minutes

Ingredients:
• 1 head of garlic, unpeeled
• 1 large eggplant, cut in half lengthwise
• 5 tablespoons olive oil
• Lemon juice to taste
• 2 minced garlic cloves
• What you'll need from the store cupboard:
• Pepper and salt to taste

Directions:
1. With the rack in the middle position, preheat oven to 350°F.
2. Line a baking sheet with parchment paper. Place the eggplant cut side down on the baking sheet.
3. Roast until the flesh is very tender and pulls away easily from the skin, about 1 hour depending on the eggplant's size. Let it cool.
4. Meanwhile, cut the tips off the garlic cloves. Place the cloves in a square of aluminum foil. Fold up the edges of the foil and crimp together to form a tightly sealed packet. Roast alongside the eggplant until tender, about 20 minutes.

Let cool.

5. Mash the cloves by pressing with a fork.

6. With a spoon, scoop the flesh from the eggplant and place it in the bowl of a food processor. Add the mashed garlic, oil and lemon juice. Process until smooth. Season with pepper.

Nutrition Info:
• Per Servings 10.2g Carbs, 1.6g Protein, 17.8g Fat, 192 Calories

Dill Pickles With Tuna-mayo Topping

Servings: 12
Cooking Time: 40 Minutes

Ingredients:
• 18 ounces canned and drained tuna
• 6 large dill pickles
• ¼ tsp garlic powder
• ⅓ cup sugar-free mayonnaise
• 1 tbsp onion flakes

Directions:
1. Combine the mayonnaise, tuna, onion flakes, and garlic powder in a bowl. Cut the pickles in half lengthwise. Top each half with tuna mixture. Place in the fridge for 30 minutes before serving.

Nutrition Info:
• Per Servings 1.5g Carbs, 11g Protein, 10g Fat, 118 Calories

Balsamic Brussels Sprouts With Prosciutto

Servings: 4
Cooking Time: 40 Minutes

Ingredients:
• 3 tbsp balsamic vinegar
• 1 tbsp erythritol
• ½ tbsp olive oil
• Salt and black pepper to taste
• 1 lb Brussels sprouts, halved
• 5 slices prosciutto, chopped

Directions:
1. Preheat oven to 400ºF and line a baking sheet with parchment paper. Mix balsamic vinegar, erythritol, olive oil, salt, and black pepper and combine with the brussels sprouts in a bowl.

2. Spread the mixture on the baking sheet and roast for 30 minutes until tender on the inside and crispy on the outside. Toss with prosciutto, share among 4 plates, and serve with chicken breasts.

Nutrition Info:
• Per Servings 0g Carbs, 8g Protein, 14g Fat, 166 Calories

Bacon Mashed Cauliflower

Servings: 6
Cooking Time: 40 Minutes

Ingredients:
• 6 slices bacon
• 3 heads cauliflower, leaves removed
• 2 cups water
• 2 tbsp melted butter
• ½ cup buttermilk
• Salt and black pepper to taste
• ¼ cup grated yellow cheddar cheese
• 2 tbsp chopped chives

Directions:
1. Preheat oven to 350ºF. Fry bacon in a heated skillet over medium heat for 5 minutes until crispy. Remove to a paper towel-lined plate, allow to cool, and crumble. Set aside and keep bacon fat.

2. Boil cauli heads in water in a pot over high heat for 7 minutes, until tender. Drain and put in a bowl.

3. Include butter, buttermilk, salt, black pepper, and puree using a hand blender until smooth and creamy. Lightly grease a casserole dish with the bacon fat and spread the mash in it.

4. Sprinkle with cheddar cheese and place under the broiler for 4 minutes on high until the cheese melts. Remove and top with bacon and chopped chives. Serve with pan-seared scallops.

Nutrition Info:
• Per Servings 6g Carbs, 14g Protein, 25g Fat, 312 Calories

Roasted String Beans, Mushrooms & Tomato Plate

Servings: 4
Cooking Time: 32 Minutes

Ingredients:
• 2 cups strings beans, cut in halves
• 1 lb cremini mushrooms, quartered
• 3 tomatoes, quartered
• 2 cloves garlic, minced
• 3 tbsp olive oil
• 3 shallots, julienned
• ½ tsp dried thyme
• Salt and black pepper to season

Directions:
1. Preheat oven to 450ºF. In a bowl, mix the strings beans, mushrooms, tomatoes, garlic, olive oil, shallots, thyme, salt, and pepper. Pour the vegetables in a baking sheet and spread them all around.

2. Place the baking sheet in the oven and bake the veggies for 20 to 25 minutes.

Nutrition Info:
- Per Servings 6g Carbs, 6g Protein, 2g Fat, 121 Calories

French Fried Butternut Squash

Servings: 6
Cooking Time: 20 Minutes

Ingredients:
- 1 medium butternut squash
- 1 tablespoon chopped fresh thyme
- 1 tablespoon chopped fresh rosemary
- 4 tablespoons olive oil
- 1/2 teaspoon salt
- Cooking spray

Directions:
1. Heat oven to 425oF. Lightly coat a baking sheet with cooking spray.
2. Peel skin from butternut squash and cut into even sticks, about 1/2-inch-wide and 3 inches long.
3. In a medium bowl, combine the squash, oil, thyme, rosemary, and salt; mix until the squash is evenly coated.
4. Spread onto the baking sheet and roast for 10 minutes.
5. Remove the baking sheet from the oven and shake to loosen the squash.
6. Return to oven and continue to roast for 10 minutes or until golden brown.
7. Serve and enjoy.

Nutrition Info:
- Per Servings 1g Carbs, 1g Protein, 9g Fat, 86 Calories

Pecorino-mushroom Balls

Servings: 4
Cooking Time: 20 Minutes

Ingredients:
- 2 tbsp butter, softened
- 2 garlic cloves, minced
- 2 cups portobello mushrooms, chopped
- 4 tbsp blanched almond flour
- 4 tbsp ground flax seeds
- 4 tbsp hemp seeds
- 4 tbsp sunflower seeds
- 1 tbsp cajun seasonings
- 1 tsp mustard
- 2 eggs, whisked
- ½ cup pecorino cheese

Directions:
1. Set a pan over medium-high heat and warm 1 tablespoon of butter. Add in mushrooms and garlic and sauté until there is no more water in mushrooms.
2. Place in pecorino cheese, almond flour, hemp seeds, mustard, eggs, sunflower seeds, flax seeds, and Cajun seasonings. Create 4 burgers from the mixture.

3. In a pan, warm the remaining butter; fry the burgers for 7 minutes. Flip them over with a wide spatula and cook for 6 more minutes. Serve while warm.

Nutrition Info:
- Per Servings 7.7g Carbs, 16.8g Protein, 30g Fat, 370 Calories

Mascarpone Snapped Amaretti Biscuits

Servings: 6
Cooking Time: 25 Minutes

Ingredients:
- 6 egg whites
- 1 egg yolk, beaten
- 1 tsp vanilla bean paste
- 8 oz swerve confectioner's sugar
- A pinch of salt
- ¼ cup ground fragrant almonds
- 1 lemon juice
- 7 tbsp sugar-free amaretto liquor
- ¼ cup mascarpone cheese
- ¼ cup butter, room temperature
- ¾ cup swerve confectioner's sugar, for topping

Directions:
1. Preheat an oven to 300ºF and line a baking sheet with parchment paper. Set aside.
2. In a bowl, beat eggs whites, salt, and vanilla paste with the hand mixer while you gradually spoon in 8 oz of swerve confectioner's sugar until a stiff mixture. Add ground almonds and fold in the egg yolk, lemon juice, and amaretto liquor. Spoon the mixture into the piping bag and press out 40 to 50 mounds on the baking sheet.
3. Bake the biscuits for 15 minutes by which time they should be golden brown. Whisk the mascarpone cheese, butter, and swerve confectioner's sugar with the cleaned electric mixer; set aside.
4. When the biscuits are ready, transfer them into a serving bowl and let cool. Spread a scoop of mascarpone cream onto one biscuit and snap with another biscuit. Sift some swerve confectioner's sugar on top of them and serve.

Nutrition Info:
- Per Servings 3g Carbs, 9g Protein, 13g Fat, 165 Calories

Vegan, Vegetable & Meatless Recipes

Vegan, Vegetable & Meatless Recipes

Sausage Roll

Servings: 6
Cooking Time: 1 Hour And 15 Minutes

Ingredients:
- 6 vegan sausages (defrosted)
- 1 cup mushrooms
- 1 onion
- 2 fresh sage leaves
- 1 package tofu skin sheet
- Salt and pepper to taste
- 5 tablespoons olive oil

Directions:
1. Preheat the oven to 180°F/356°F assisted.
2. Defrost the vegan sausages.
3. Roughly chop the mushrooms and add them to a food processor. Process until mostly broken down. Peel and roughly chop the onions, then add them to the processor along with the defrosted vegan sausages, sage leaves, and a pinch of salt and pepper. Pour in the oil. Process until all the ingredients have mostly broken down, and only a few larger pieces remain.
4. Heat a frying pan on a medium heat. Once hot, transfer the mushroom mixture to the pan and fry for 20 minutes or until almost all of the moisture has evaporated, frequently stirring to prevent the mixture sticking to the pan.
5. Remove the mushroom mixture from the heat and transfer to a plate. Leave to cool completely. Tip: if it's cold outside, we leave the mushroom mixture outdoors, so it cools quicker.
6. Meanwhile, either line a large baking tray with baking paper or (if the pastry already comes wrapped in a sheet of baking paper) roll out the tofu skin onto the tray and cut it in half both lengthways and widthways to create 4 equal-sized pieces of tofu skin.
7. Spoon a quarter of the mushroom mixture along the length of each rectangle of tofu skin and shape the mixture into a log. Add one vegan sausage and roll into a log.
8. Seal the roll by securing the edged with a toothpick.
9. Brush the sausage rolls with olive oil and bake for 40-45 minutes until golden brown. Enjoy!

Nutrition Info:
- Per Servings 3g Carbs, 0.9g Protein, 11g Fat, 113 Calories

Walnuts With Tofu

Servings: 4
Cooking Time: 13 Minutes

Ingredients:
- 3 tsp olive oil
- 1 cup extra firm tofu, cubed
- ¼ cup walnuts, chopped
- 1 ½ tbsp coconut aminos
- 3 tbsp vegetable broth
- ½ tsp smashed garlic
- 1 tsp cayenne pepper
- ½ tsp turmeric powder
- Sea salt and black pepper, to taste
- 2 tsp sunflower seeds

Directions:
1. Set a frying pan over medium heat. Warm the oil. Add in tofu and fry as you stir until they brown. Pour in the walnuts; turn temperature to higher and cook for 2 minutes. Stir in the remaining ingredients, set heat to medium-low and cook for 5 more minutes. Drizzle with hot sauce and serve!

Nutrition Info:
- Per Servings 5.3g Carbs, 8.3g Protein, 21.6g Fat, 232 Calories

Grilled Spicy Eggplant

Servings: 2
Cooking Time: 20 Minutes

Ingredients:
- 2 small eggplants, cut into 1/2-inch slices
- 1/4 cup olive oil
- 2 tablespoons lime juice
- 3 teaspoons Cajun seasoning
- Salt and pepper to taste

Directions:
1. Brush eggplant slices with oil. Drizzle with lime juice; sprinkle with Cajun seasoning. Let stand for 5 minutes.
2. Grill eggplant, covered, over medium heat or broil 4 minutes. from heat until tender, 4-5 minutes per side.
3. Season with pepper and salt to taste.
4. Serve and enjoy.

Nutrition Info:
- Per Servings 7g Carbs, 5g Protein, 28g Fat, 350 Calories

Keto Cauliflower Hash Browns

Servings: 4
Cooking Time: 30 Mins

Ingredients:
- 1 lb cauliflower
- 3 eggs
- ½ yellow onion, grated
- 2 pinches pepper
- 4 oz. butter, for frying
- What you'll need from the store cupboard:
- 1 tsp salt

Directions:
1. Rinse, trim and grate the cauliflower using a food processor or grater.
2. In a large bowl, add the cauliflower onion and pepper, tossing evenly. Set aside for 5 to 10 minutes.
3. In a large skillet over medium heat, heat a generous amount of butter on medium heat. The cooking process will go quicker if you plan to have room for 3–4 pancakes at a time. Use the oven on low heat to keep the first batches of pancakes warm while you make the others.
4. Place scoops of the grated cauliflower mixture in the frying pan and flatten them carefully until they measure about 3 to 4 inches in diameter.
5. Fry for 4 to 5 minutes on each side. Adjust the heat to make sure they don't burn. Serve.

Nutrition Info:
- Per Servings 5g Carbs, 7g Protein, 26g Fat, 282 Calories

Cremini Mushroom Stroganoff

Servings: 4
Cooking Time: 15 Minutes

Ingredients:
- 3 tbsp butter
- 1 white onion, chopped
- 4 cups cremini mushrooms, cubed
- 2 cups water
- ½ cup heavy cream
- ½ cup grated Parmesan cheese
- 1 ½ tbsp dried mixed herbs
- Salt and black pepper to taste

Directions:
1. Melt the butter in a saucepan over medium heat, sauté the onion for 3 minutes until soft.
2. Stir in the mushrooms and cook until tender, about 3 minutes. Add the water, mix, and bring to boil for 4 minutes until the water reduces slightly.
3. Pour in the heavy cream and parmesan cheese. Stir to melt the cheese. Also, mix in the dried herbs. Season with salt and pepper, simmer for 40 seconds and turn the heat off.

4. Ladle stroganoff over a bed of spaghetti squash and serve.

Nutrition Info:
- Per Servings 1g Carbs, 5g Protein, 28g Fat, 284 Calories

Garlic Lemon Mushrooms

Servings: 4
Cooking Time: 20 Minutes

Ingredients:
- 1/4 cup lemon juice
- 3 tablespoons minced fresh parsley
- 3 garlic cloves, minced
- 1-pound large fresh mushrooms
- 4 tablespoons olive oil
- Pepper to taste

Directions:
1. For the dressing, whisk together the first 5 ingredients. Toss mushrooms with 2 tablespoons dressing.
2. Grill mushrooms, covered, over medium-high heat until tender, 5-7 minutes per side. Toss with remaining dressing before serving.

Nutrition Info:
- Per Servings 6.8g Carbs, 4g Protein, 14g Fat, 160 Calories

Pumpkin Bake

Servings: 6
Cooking Time: 45 Minutes

Ingredients:
- 3 large Pumpkins, peeled and sliced
- 1 cup almond flour
- 1 cup grated mozzarella cheese
- 2 tbsp olive oil
- ½ cup chopped parsley

Directions:
1. Preheat the oven to 350ºF. Arrange the pumpkin slices in a baking dish, drizzle with olive oil, and bake for 35 minutes. Mix the almond flour, cheese, and parsley and when the pumpkin is ready, remove it from the oven, and sprinkle the cheese mixture all over. Place back in the oven and grill the top for 5 minutes.

Nutrition Info:
- Per Servings 5.7g Carbs, 2.7g Protein, 4.8g Fat, 125 Calories

Greek Styled Veggie-rice

Servings: 3
Cooking Time: 20 Minutes

Ingredients:
- 3 tbsp chopped fresh mint
- 1 small tomato, chopped
- 1 head cauliflower, cut into large florets
- ¼ cup fresh lemon juice
- ½ yellow onion, minced
- pepper and salt to taste
- ¼ cup extra virgin olive oil

Directions:
1. In a bowl, mix lemon juice and onion and leave for 30 minutes. Then drain onion and reserve the juice and onion bits.
2. In a blender, shred cauliflower until the size of a grain of rice.
3. On medium fire, place a medium nonstick skillet and for 8-10 minutes cook cauliflower while covered.
4. Add grape tomatoes and cook for 3 minutes while stirring occasionally.
5. Add mint and onion bits. Cook for another three minutes.
6. Meanwhile, in a small bowl whisk pepper, salt, 3 tbsp reserved lemon juice, and olive oil until well blended.
7. Remove cooked cauliflower, transfer to a serving bowl, pour lemon juice mixture, and toss to mix.
8. Before serving, if needed season with pepper and salt to taste.

Nutrition Info:
- Per Servings 4.0g Carbs, 2.3g Protein, 9.5g Fat, 120 Calories

Grilled Cheese The Keto Way

Servings: 1
Cooking Time: 15 Minutes

Ingredients:
- 2 eggs
- ½ tsp baking powder
- 2 tbsp butter
- 2 tbsp almond flour
- 1 ½ tbsp psyllium husk powder
- 2 ounces cheddar cheese

Directions:
1. Whisk together all ingredients except 1 tbsp. butter and cheddar cheese. Place in a square oven-proof bowl, and microwave for 90 seconds. Flip the bun over and cut in half.
2. Place the cheddar cheese on one half of the bun and top with the other. Melt the remaining butter in a skillet. Add the sandwich and grill until the cheese is melted and the bun is crispy.

Nutrition Info:
- Per Servings 6.1g Carbs, 25g Protein, 51g Fat, 623 Calories

Portobello Mushroom Burgers

Servings: 4
Cooking Time: 15 Minutes

Ingredients:
- 4 low carb buns
- 4 portobello mushroom caps
- 1 clove garlic, minced
- ½ tsp salt
- 2 tbsp olive oil
- ½ cup sliced roasted red peppers
- 2 medium tomatoes, chopped
- ¼ cup crumbled feta cheese
- 1 tbsp red wine vinegar
- 2 tbsp pitted kalamata olives, chopped
- ½ tsp dried oregano
- 2 cups baby salad greens

Directions:
1. Heat the grill pan over medium-high heat and while it heats, crush the garlic with salt in a bowl using the back of a spoon. Stir in 1 tablespoon of oil and brush the mushrooms and each inner side of the buns with the mixture.
2. Place the mushrooms in the heated pan and grill them on both sides for 8 minutes until tender.
3. Also, toast the buns in the pan until they are crisp, about 2 minutes. Set aside.
4. In a bowl, mix the red peppers, tomatoes, olives, feta cheese, vinegar, oregano, baby salad greens, and remaining oil; toss them. Assemble the burger: in a slice of bun, add a mushroom cap, a scoop of vegetables, and another slice of bread. Serve with cheese dip.

Nutrition Info:
- Per Servings 3g Carbs, 16g Protein, 8g Fat, 190 Calories

Cilantro-lime Guacamole

Servings: 4
Cooking Time: 10 Minutes

Ingredients:
- 3 avocados, peeled, pitted, and mashed
- 1 lime, juiced
- 1/2 cup diced onion
- 3 tablespoons chopped fresh cilantro
- 2 Roma (plum) tomatoes, diced
- 1 teaspoon salt
- 1 teaspoon minced garlic
- 1 pinch ground cayenne pepper (optional)
- 1 teaspoon minced garlic

Directions:
1. In a mixing bowl, mash the avocados with a fork. Sprinkle with salt and lime juice.
2. Stir together diced onion, tomatoes, cilantro, pepper and garlic.
3. Serve immediately, or refrigerate until ready to serve.

Nutrition Info:
- Per Servings 8g Carbs, 19g Protein, 22.2g Fat, 362 Calories

Cauliflower & Mushrooms Stuffed Peppers

Servings: 4
Cooking Time: 40 Minutes

Ingredients:
- 1 head cauliflower
- 4 bell peppers
- 1 cup mushrooms, sliced
- 1 ½ tbsp oil
- 1 onion, chopped
- 1 cup celery, chopped
- 1 garlic cloves, minced
- 1 tsp chili powder
- 2 tomatoes, pureed
- Sea salt and pepper, to taste

Directions:
1. To prepare cauliflower rice, grate the cauliflower into rice-size. Set in a kitchen towel to attract and remove any excess moisture. Set oven to 360ºF.
2. Lightly oil a casserole dish. Chop off bell pepper tops, do away with the seeds and core. Line a baking pan with a parchment paper and roast the peppers for 18 minutes until the skin starts to brown.
3. Warm the oil over medium heat. Add in garlic, celery, and onion and sauté until soft and translucent. Stir in chili powder, mushrooms, and cauliflower rice. Cook for 6 minutes until the cauliflower rice becomes tender. Split the cauliflower mixture among the bell peppers. Set in the casserole dish. Combine pepper, salt, and tomatoes. Top the peppers with the tomato mixture. Bake for 10 minutes.

Nutrition Info:
- Per Servings 8.4g Carbs, 1.6g Protein, 4.8g Fat, 77 Calories

Morning Granola

Servings: 8
Cooking Time: 1 Hour

Ingredients:
- 1 tbsp coconut oil
- ⅓ cup almond flakes
- ½ cups almond milk
- 2 tbsp sugar
- 1/8 tsp salt
- 1 tsp lime zest
- 1/8 tsp nutmeg, grated
- ½ tsp ground cinnamon
- ½ cup pecans, chopped
- ½ cup almonds, slivered
- 2 tbsp pepitas
- 3 tbsp sunflower seeds
- ¼ cup flax seed

Directions:
1. Set a deep pan over medium-high heat and warm the coconut oil. Add almond flakes and toast for 1 to 2 minutes. Stir in the remaining ingredients. Set oven to 300ºF. Lay the mixture in an even layer onto a baking sheet lined with a parchment paper. Bake for 1 hour, making sure that you shake gently in intervals of 15 minutes. Serve alongside additional almond milk.

Nutrition Info:
- Per Servings 9.2g Carbs, 5.1g Protein, 24.3g Fat, 262 Calories

Creamy Artichoke And Spinach

Servings: 4
Cooking Time: 15 Minutes

Ingredients:
- 5 tablespoons olive oil
- 1 can water-packed artichoke hearts quartered
- 1 package frozen spinach
- 1 cup shredded part-skim mozzarella cheese, divided
- 1/4 cup grated Parmesan cheese
- 1/2 teaspoon salt
- 1/4 teaspoon pepper

Directions:
1. Heat oil in a pan over medium flame. Add artichoke hearts and season with salt and pepper to taste. Cook for 5 minutes. Stir in the spinach until wilted.
2. Place in a bowl and stir in mozzarella cheese, Parmesan cheese, salt, and pepper. Toss to combine.
3. Transfer to a greased 2-qt. Broiler-safe baking dish; sprinkle with remaining mozzarella cheese. Broil 4-6 in. from heat 2-3 minutes or until cheese is melted.

Nutrition Info:
- Per Servings 7.3g Carbs, 11.5g Protein, 23.9g Fat, 283 Calories

Bell Pepper & Pumpkin With Avocado Sauce

Servings: 4
Cooking Time: 15 Minutes

Ingredients:
- ½ pound pumpkin, peeled
- ½ pound bell peppers
- 1 tbsp olive oil
- 1 avocado, peeled and pitted
- 1 lemon, juiced and zested
- 2 tbsp sesame oil
- 2 tbsp cilantro, chopped
- 1 onion, chopped
- 1 jalapeño pepper, deveined and minced
- Salt and black pepper, to taste

Directions:
1. Use a spiralizer to spiralize bell peppers and pumpkin. Using a large nonstick skillet, warm olive oil. Add in bell peppers and pumpkin and sauté for 8 minutes.
2. Combine the remaining ingredients to obtain a creamy mixture. Top the vegetable noodles with the avocado sauce and serve.

Nutrition Info:
- Per Servings 11g Carbs, 1.9g Protein, 20.2g Fat, 233 Calories

Greek-style Zucchini Pasta

Servings: 4
Cooking Time: 15 Minutes

Ingredients:
- ¼ cup sun-dried tomatoes
- 5 garlic cloves, minced
- 2 tbsp butter
- 1 cup spinach
- 2 large zucchinis, spiralized
- ¼ cup crumbled feta
- ¼ cup Parmesan cheese, shredded
- 10 kalamata olives, halved
- 2 tbsp olive oil
- 2 tbsp chopped parsley

Directions:
1. Heat the olive oil in a pan over medium heat. Add zoodles, butter, garlic, and spinach. Cook for about 5 minutes. Stir in the olives, tomatoes, and parsley. Cook for 2 more minutes. Add in the cheeses and serve.

Nutrition Info:
- Per Servings 6.5g Carbs, 6.5g Protein, 19.5g Fat, 231 Calories

Herb Butter With Parsley

Servings: 1
Cooking Time: 0 Minutes

Ingredients:
- 5 oz. butter, at room temperature
- 1 garlic clove, pressed
- ½ tbsp garlic powder
- 4 tbsp fresh parsley, finely chopped
- 1 tsp lemon juice
- ½ tsp salt

Directions:
1. In a bowl, stir all ingredients until completely combined. Set aside for 15 minutes or refrigerate it before serving.

Nutrition Info:
- Per Servings 1g Carbs, 1g Protein, 28g Fat, 258 Calories

Onion & Nuts Stuffed Mushrooms

Servings: 4
Cooking Time: 30 Minutes

Ingredients:
- 1 tbsp sesame oil
- 1 onion, chopped
- 1 garlic clove, minced
- 1 pound mushrooms, stems removed
- Salt and black pepper, to taste
- ¼ cup raw pine nuts
- 2 tbsp parsley, chopped

Directions:
1. Set oven to 360°F. Use a nonstick cooking spray to grease a large baking sheet. Into a frying pan, add sesame oil and warm. Place in garlic and onion and cook until soft.
2. Chop the mushroom stems and cook until tender. Turn off the heat, sprinkle with pepper and salt; add in pine nuts. Take the nut/mushroom mixture and stuff them to the mushroom caps and set on the baking sheet.
3. Bake the stuffed mushrooms for 30 minutes and remove to a wire rack to cool slightly. Add fresh parsley for garnish and serve.

Nutrition Info:
- Per Servings 7.4g Carbs, 4.8g Protein, 11.2g Fat, 139 Calories

Cream Of Zucchini And Avocado

Servings: 4
Cooking Time: 35 Minutes

Ingredients:
- 3 tsp vegetable oil
- 1 onion, chopped
- 1 carrot, sliced
- 1 turnip, sliced
- 3 cups zucchinis, chopped
- 1 avocado, peeled and diced
- ¼ tsp ground black pepper
- 4 vegetable broth
- 1 tomato, pureed

Directions:
1. In a pot, warm the oil and sauté onion until translucent, about 3 minutes. Add in turnip, zucchini, and carrot and cook for 7 minutes; add black pepper for seasoning.
2. Mix in pureed tomato, and broth; and boil. Change heat to low and allow the mixture to simmer for 20 minutes. Lift from the heat. In batches, add the soup and avocado to a blender. Blend until creamy and smooth.

Nutrition Info:
- Per Servings 11g Carbs, 2.2g Protein, 13.4g Fat, 165 Calories

Mushroom & Cauliflower Bake

Servings: 4
Cooking Time: 30 Minutes

Ingredients:
- Cooking spray
- 1 head cauliflower, cut into florets
- 8 ounces mushrooms, halved
- 2 garlic cloves, smashed
- 2 tomatoes, pureed
- ¼ cup coconut oil, melted
- 1 tsp chili paprika paste
- ¼ tsp marjoram
- ½ tsp curry powder
- Salt and black pepper, to taste

Directions:
1. Set oven to 390°F. Apply a cooking spray to a baking dish. Lay mushrooms and cauliflower in the baking dish. Around the vegetables, scatter smashed garlic. Place in the pureed tomatoes. Sprinkle over melted coconut oil and place in chili paprika paste, curry, black pepper, salt, and marjoram. Roast for 25 minutes, turning once. Place in a serving plate and serve with green salad.

Nutrition Info:
- Per Servings 11.6g Carbs, 5g Protein, 6.7g Fat, 113 Calories

Cauliflower Risotto With Mushrooms

Servings: 4
Cooking Time: 15 Minutes

Ingredients:
- 2 shallots, diced
- 3 tbsp olive oil
- ¼ cup veggie broth
- ⅓ cup Parmesan cheese
- 4 tbsp butter
- 3 tbsp chopped chives
- 2 pounds mushrooms, sliced
- 4 ½ cups riced cauliflower

Directions:
1. Heat 2 tbsp. oil in a saucepan. Add the mushrooms and cook over medium heat for about 3 minutes. Remove from the pan and set aside.
2. Heat the remaining oil and cook the shallots for 2 minutes. Stir in the cauliflower and broth, and cook until the liquid is absorbed. Stir in the rest of the ingredients.

Nutrition Info:
- Per Servings 8.4g Carbs, 11g Protein, 18g Fat, 264 Calories

Paprika 'n Cajun Seasoned Onion Rings

Servings: 6
Cooking Time: 25 Minutes

Ingredients:
- 1 large white onion
- 2 large eggs, beaten
- ½ teaspoon Cajun seasoning
- ¾ cup almond flour
- 1 ½ teaspoon paprika
- ½ cups coconut oil for frying
- ¼ cup water
- Salt and pepper to taste

Directions:
1. Preheat a pot with oil for 8 minutes.
2. Peel the onion, cut off the top and slice into circles.
3. In a mixing bowl, combine the water and the eggs. Season with pepper and salt.
4. Soak the onion in the egg mixture.
5. In another bowl, combine the almond flour, paprika powder, Cajun seasoning, salt and pepper.
6. Dredge the onion in the almond flour mixture.
7. Place in the pot and cook in batches until golden brown, around 8 minutes per batch.

Nutrition Info:
- Per Servings 3.9g Carbs, 2.8g Protein, 24.1g Fat, 262 Calories

Stuffed Cremini Mushrooms

Servings: 4
Cooking Time: 35 Minutes

Ingredients:
- ½ head broccoli, cut into florets
- 1 pound cremini mushrooms, stems removed
- 2 tbsp coconut oil
- 1 onion, finely chopped
- 1 tsp garlic, minced
- 1 bell pepper, chopped
- 1 tsp cajun seasoning mix
- Salt and black pepper, to taste
- 1 cup vegan cheese

Directions:
1. Use a food processor to pulse broccoli florets until become like small rice-like granules.
2. Set oven to 360ºF. Bake mushroom caps until tender for 8 to 12 minutes. In a heavy-bottomed skillet, melt the oil; stir in bell pepper, garlic, and onion and sauté until fragrant. Place in pepper, salt, and cajun seasoning mix. Fold in broccoli rice.
3. Equally separate the filling mixture among mushroom caps. Add a topping of vegan cheese and bake for 17 more minutes. Serve warm.

Nutrition Info:
- Per Servings 10g Carbs, 12.7g Protein, 13.4g Fat, 206 Calories

Wild Mushroom And Asparagus Stew

Servings: 4
Cooking Time: 25 Minutes

Ingredients:
- 2 tbsp olive oil
- 1 cup onions, chopped
- 2 garlic cloves, pressed
- ½ cup celery, chopped
- 2 carrots, chopped
- 1 cup wild mushrooms, sliced
- 2 tbsp dry white wine
- 2 rosemary sprigs, chopped
- 1 thyme sprig, chopped
- 4 cups vegetable stock
- ½ tsp chili pepper
- 1 tsp smoked paprika
- 2 tomatoes, chopped
- 1 tbsp flax seed meal

Directions:
1. Set a stockpot over medium heat and warm oil. Add in onions and cook until tender.
2. Place in carrots, celery, and garlic and cook until soft for 4 more minutes. Add in mushrooms; cook the mixture the liquid is lost; set the vegetables aside. Stir in wine to deglaze the stockpot's bottom. Place in thyme and rosemary. Pour in tomatoes, vegetable stock, paprika, and chili pepper; add in reserved vegetables and allow to boil.
3. On low heat, allow the mixture to simmer for 15 minutes while covered. Stir in flax seed meal to thicken the stew. Plate into individual bowls and serve.

Nutrition Info:
- Per Servings 9.5g Carbs, 2.1g Protein, 7.3g Fat, 114 Calories

Walnut Tofu Sauté

Servings: 4
Cooking Time: 15 Minutes

Ingredients:
- 1 tbsp olive oil
- 1 block firm tofu, cubed
- 1 tbsp tomato paste with garlic and onion
- 1 tbsp balsamic vinegar
- Pink salt and black pepper to taste
- ½ tsp mixed dried herbs
- 1 cup chopped raw walnuts

Directions:
1. Heat the oil in a skillet over medium heat and cook the tofu for 3 minutes while stirring to brown.
2. Mix the tomato paste with the vinegar and add to the tofu. Stir, season with salt and black pepper, and cook for another 4 minutes.
3. Add the herbs and walnuts. Stir and cook on low heat for 3 minutes to be fragrant. Spoon to a side of squash mash and a sweet berry sauce to serve.

Nutrition Info:
- Per Servings 4g Carbs, 18g Protein, 24g Fat, 320 Calories

Bell Pepper Stuffed Avocado

Servings: 8
Cooking Time: 10 Minutes

Ingredients:
- 4 avocados, pitted and halved
- 2 tbsp olive oil
- 3 cups green bell peppers, chopped
- 1 onion, chopped
- 1 tsp garlic puree
- Salt and black pepper, to taste
- 1 tsp deli mustard
- 1 tomato, chopped

Directions:
1. From each half of the avocados, scoop out 2 teaspoons of flesh; set aside.
2. Use a sauté pan to warm oil over medium-high heat. Cook the garlic, onion, and bell peppers until tender. Mix in the reserved avocado. Add in tomato, salt, mustard, and black pepper. Separate the mushroom mixture and mix equally among the avocado halves and serve.

Nutrition Info:
- Per Servings 7.4g Carbs, 2.4g Protein, 23.2g Fat, 255 Calories

Keto Pizza Margherita

Servings: 2
Cooking Time: 40 Minutes

Ingredients:
- 6 ounces mozzarella
- 2 tbsp cream cheese
- 2 tbsp Parmesan cheese
- 1 tsp oregano
- ½ cup almond flour
- 2 tbsp psyllium husk
- Topping
- 4 ounces grated cheddar cheese
- ¼ cup Marinara sauce
- 1 bell pepper, sliced
- 1 tomato, sliced
- 2 tbsp chopped basil

Directions:
1. Preheat the oven to 400ºF. Combine all crust ingredients in a large bowl, except the mozzarella.
2. Melt the mozzarella in a microwave. Stir it into the bowl. Mix with your hands to combine. Divide the dough in two. Roll out the two crusts in circles and place on a lined baking sheet. Bake for about 10 minutes. Top with the toppings. Return to the oven and bake for another 10 minutes.

Nutrition Info:
- Per Servings 3.7g Carbs, 31g Protein, 39g Fat, 510 Calories

Garlic And Greens

Servings: 4
Cooking Time: 20 Minutes

Ingredients:
- 1-pound kale, trimmed and torn
- 1/4 cup chopped oil-packed sun-dried tomatoes
- 5 garlic cloves, minced
- 2 tablespoons minced fresh parsley
- 1/4 teaspoon salt
- 3 tablespoons olive oil

Directions:
1. In a 6-qt. stockpot, bring 1 inch. of water to a boil. Add kale; cook, covered, 10-15 minutes or until tender. Remove with a slotted spoon; discard cooking liquid.
2. In the same pot, heat oil over medium heat. Add tomatoes and garlic; cook and stir 1 minute. Add kale, parsley and salt; heat through, stirring occasionally.

Nutrition Info:
- Per Servings 9g Carbs, 6g Protein, 13g Fat, 160 Calories

Coconut Cauliflower & Parsnip Soup

Servings: 4
Cooking Time: 20 Minutes

Ingredients:
- 4 cups vegetable broth
- 2 heads cauliflower, cut into florets
- 1 cup parsnip, chopped
- 1 tbsp coconut oil
- 1 cup coconut milk
- ½ tsp red pepper flakes

Directions:

1. Add water in a pot set over medium-high heat and bring to a boil. Add in cauliflower florets and parsnip, cook for about 10 minutes. Add in broth and coconut oil. While on low heat, cook for an additional 5 minutes. Transfer the mixture to an immersion blender and puree.

2. Plate into four separate soup bowls; decorate each with red pepper flakes. Serve while warm.

Nutrition Info:
- Per Servings 7g Carbs, 2.7g Protein, 7.2g Fat, 94 Calories

Classic Tangy Ratatouille

Servings: 6
Cooking Time: 47 Minutes

Ingredients:
- 2 eggplants, chopped
- 3 zucchinis, chopped
- 2 red onions, diced
- 1 can tomatoes
- 2 red bell peppers, cut in chunks
- 1 yellow bell pepper, cut in chunks
- 3 cloves garlic, sliced
- ½ cup basil leaves, chop half
- 4 sprigs thyme
- 1 tbsp balsamic vinegar
- 2 tbsp olive oil
- ½ lemon, zested

Directions:

1. In a casserole pot, heat the olive oil and sauté the eggplants, zucchinis, and bell peppers over medium heat for 5 minutes. Spoon the veggies into a large bowl.

2. In the same pan, sauté garlic, onions, and thyme leaves for 5 minutes and return the cooked veggies to the pan along with the canned tomatoes, balsamic vinegar, chopped basil, salt, and pepper to taste. Stir and cover the pot, and cook the ingredients on low heat for 30 minutes.

3. Open the lid and stir in the remaining basil leaves, lemon zest, and adjust the seasoning. Turn the heat off. Plate the ratatouille and serve with some low carb crusted bread.

Nutrition Info:
- Per Servings 5.6g Carbs, 1.7g Protein, 12.1g Fat, 154 Calories

Garlicky Bok Choy

Servings: 4
Cooking Time: 25 Minutes

Ingredients:
- 2 pounds bok choy, chopped
- 2 tbsp almond oil
- 1 tsp garlic, minced
- ½ tsp thyme
- ½ tsp red pepper flakes, crushed
- Salt and black pepper, to the taste

Directions:

1. Add Bok choy in a pot containing salted water and cook for 10 minutes over medium heat. Drain and set aside. Place a sauté pan over medium-high heat and warm the oil.

2. Add in garlic and cook until soft. Stir in the Bok choy, red pepper, black pepper, salt, and thyme and ensure they are heated through. Add more seasonings if needed and serve warm with cauli rice.

Nutrition Info:
- Per Servings 13.4g Carbs, 2.9g Protein, 7g Fat, 118 Calories

Soups, Stew & Salads Recipes

Soups, Stew & Salads Recipes

Traditional Greek Salad

Servings: 4
Cooking Time: 10 Minutes

Ingredients:
- 5 tomatoes, chopped
- 1 large cucumber, chopped
- 1 green bell pepper, chopped
- 1 small red onion, chopped
- 16 kalamata olives, chopped
- 4 tbsp capers
- 1 cup feta cheese, chopped
- 1 tsp oregano, dried
- 4 tbsp olive oil
- Salt to taste

Directions:
1. Place tomatoes, bell pepper, cucumber, onion, feta cheese and olives in a bowl; mix to combine well. Season with salt. Combine capers, olive oil, and oregano, in a small bowl. Drizzle with the dressing to serve.

Nutrition Info:
- Per Servings 8g Carbs, 9.3g Protein, 28g Fat, 323 Calories

Bacon Chowder

Servings: 6
Cooking Time: 15 Minutes

Ingredients:
- 1-pound bacon strips, chopped
- 1/4 cup chopped onion
- 1 can evaporated milk
- 1 sprig parsley, chopped
- 5 tablespoons butter
- 1/4 teaspoon salt
- 1/4 teaspoon pepper

Directions:
1. In a large skillet, cook bacon over medium heat until crisp, stirring occasionally. Remove with a slotted spoon; drain on paper towels. Discard drippings, reserving 1-1/2 teaspoons in the pan. Add onion to drippings; cook and stir over medium-high heat until tender.
2. Meanwhile, place all ingredients Bring to a boil over high heat. Reduce heat to medium; cook, uncovered, 10-15 minutes or until tender. Reserve 1 cup potato water.
3. Add milk, salt and pepper to the saucepan; heat through. Stir in bacon and onion.

Nutrition Info:
- Per Servings 5.4g Carbs, 10g Protein, 31.9g Fat, 322 Calories

Warm Baby Artichoke Salad

Servings: 4
Cooking Time: 30 Minutes

Ingredients:
- 6 baby artichokes
- 6 cups water
- 1 tbsp lemon juice
- ¼ cup cherry peppers, halved
- ¼ cup pitted olives, sliced
- ¼ cup olive oil
- ¼ tsp lemon zest
- 2 tsp balsamic vinegar, sugar-free
- 1 tbsp chopped dill
- ½ tsp salt
- ¼ tsp black pepper
- 1 tbsp capers
- ¼ tsp caper brine

Directions:
1. Combine the water and salt in a pot over medium heat. Trim and halve the artichokes; add to the pot. Bring to a boil, lower the heat, and let simmer for 20 minutes until tender.
2. Combine the rest of the ingredients, except the olives in a bowl. Drain and place the artichokes in a serving plate. Pour the prepared mixture over; toss to combine well. Serve topped with the olives.

Nutrition Info:
- Per Servings 5g Carbs, 1g Protein, 13g Fat, 170 Calories

Chicken And Cauliflower Rice Soup

Servings: 8
Cooking Time: 20 Mins

Ingredients:
- 2 cooked, boneless chicken breast halves, shredded
- 2 packages Steamed Cauliflower Rice
- 1/4 cup celery, chopped
- 1/2 cup onion, chopped
- 4 garlic cloves, minced
- Salt and ground black pepper to taste
- 2 teaspoons poultry seasoning
- 4 cups chicken broth

- ½ cup butter
- 2 cups heavy cream

Directions:

1. Heat butter in a large pot over medium heat, add onion, celery and garlic cloves to cook until tender. Meanwhile, place the riced cauliflower steam bags in the microwave following directions on the package.
2. Add the riced cauliflower, seasoning, salt and black pepper to butter mixture, saute them for 7 minutes on medium heat, stirring constantly to well combined.
3. Bring cooked chicken breast halves, broth and heavy cream to a broil. When it starts boiling, lower the heat, cover and simmer for 15 minutes.

Nutrition Info:

- Per Servings 6g Carbs, 27g Protein, 30g Fat, 415 Calories

Shrimp With Avocado & Cauliflower Salad

Servings: 6
Cooking Time: 30 Minutes

Ingredients:

- 1 cauliflower head, florets only
- 1 pound medium shrimp
- ¼ cup + 1 tbsp olive oil
- 1 avocado, chopped
- 3 tbsp chopped dill
- ¼ cup lemon juice
- 2 tbsp lemon zest
- Salt and black pepper to taste

Directions:

1. Heat 1 tbsp olive oil in a skillet and cook the shrimp until opaque, about 8-10 minutes. Place the cauliflower florets in a microwave-safe bowl, and microwave for 5 minutes. Place the shrimp, cauliflower, and avocado in a large bowl.
2. Whisk together the remaining olive oil, lemon zest, juice, dill, and some salt and pepper, in another bowl. Pour the dressing over, toss to combine and serve immediately.

Nutrition Info:

- Per Servings 5g Carbs, 15g Protein, 17g Fat, 214 Calories

Creamy Soup With Greens

Servings: 6
Cooking Time: 20 Minutes

Ingredients:

- ½-pounds collard greens, torn to bite-sized pieces
- 5 cups chicken broth
- 2 cups broccoli florets
- 1 cup diced onion
- 3 tablespoon oil

- 4 tablespoons butter
- Salt and pepper to taste

Directions:

1. Add all ingredients to the pot and bring to a boil.
2. Lower fire to a simmer and simmer for 15 minutes while covered.
3. With an immersion blender, puree soup until creamy.
4. Adjust seasoning to taste.
5. Serve and enjoy.

Nutrition Info:

- Per Servings 6.5g Carbs, 50.6g Protein, 33.5g Fat, 548 Calories

Creamy Squash Bisque

Servings: 8
Cooking Time: 25 Minutes

Ingredients:

- ½ tablespoon turmeric powder
- ½ teaspoon cumin
- ½ cup onion, chopped
- 2 medium-sized kabocha squash, seeded and chopped
- 1 cup coconut milk
- 3 tablespoons oil
- 1 cup water
- Pepper and salt to taste

Directions:

1. Place a heavy-bottomed pot on medium-high fire and heat for 3 minutes.
2. Add oil to the pot and swirl to coat sides and bottom of the pot. Heat for 2 minutes.
3. Place squash in a single layer and season generously with pepper and salt.
4. Sprinkle turmeric, cumin, and onion. Add water.
5. Cover and bring to a boil. Once boiling, lower fire to a simmer and let it cook for 10 minutes.
6. With a handheld blender, puree squash. Stir in coconut milk and mix well. Cook until heated through, around 5 minutes.
7. Serve and enjoy.

Nutrition Info:

- Per Servings 10.9g Carbs, 3.1g Protein, 18.1g Fat, 218 Calories

Brazilian Moqueca (shrimp Stew)

Servings: 6
Cooking Time: 25 Minutes

Ingredients:

- 1 cup coconut milk
- 2 tbsp lime juice
- ¼ cup diced roasted peppers
- 1 ½ pounds shrimp, peeled and deveined

- ¼ cup olive oil
- 1 garlic clove, minced
- 14 ounces diced tomatoes
- 2 tbsp sriracha sauce
- 1 chopped onion
- ¼ cup chopped cilantro
- Fresh dill, chopped to garnish
- Salt and black pepper, to taste

Directions:

1. Heat the olive oil in a pot over medium heat. Add onion and cook for 3 minutes or until translucent. Add the garlic and cook for another minute, until soft. Add tomatoes, shrimp, and cilantro. Cook until the shrimp becomes opaque, about 3-4 minutes.

2. Stir in sriracha sauce and coconut milk, and cook for 2 minutes. Do not bring to a boil. Stir in the lime juice and season with salt and pepper. Spoon the stew in bowls, garnish with fresh dill to serve.

Nutrition Info:

- Per Servings 5g Carbs, 23.1g Protein, 21g Fat, 324 Calories

Broccoli Slaw Salad With Mustard-mayo Dressing

Servings: 6
Cooking Time: 10 Minutes

Ingredients:

- 2 tbsp granulated swerve
- 1 tbsp Dijon mustard
- 1 tbsp olive oil
- 4 cups broccoli slaw
- ⅓ cup mayonnaise, sugar-free
- 1 tsp celery seeds
- 1 ½ tbsp apple cider vinegar
- Salt and black pepper, to taste

Directions:

1. Whisk together all ingredients except the broccoli slaw. Place broccoli slaw in a large salad bowl. Pour the dressing over. Mix with your hands to combine well.

Nutrition Info:

- Per Servings 2g Carbs, 3g Protein, 10g Fat, 110 Calories

Green Salad

Servings: 4
Cooking Time: 30 Minutes

Ingredients:

- 2 cups green beans, chopped
- 2 cups shredded spinach
- ½ cup parmesan cheese
- 3 cups basil leaves
- 3 cloves of garlic

- Salt to taste
- ¼ cup olive oil

Directions:

1. Heat a little olive oil in a skillet over medium heat and add the green beans and season with salt to taste. Sauté for 3 to 5 minutes.

2. Place the green beans in a bowl and add in the spinach.

3. In a food processor, combine half of the parmesan cheese, basil, and garlic. Add in the rest of the oil and season with salt and pepper to taste.

4. Pour into the green beans and toss to coat the ingredients.

Nutrition Info:

- Per Servings 6g Carbs, 5g Protein, 17g Fat, 196 Calories

Citrusy Brussels Sprouts Salad

Servings: 6
Cooking Time: 3 Minutes

Ingredients:

- 2 tablespoons olive oil
- ¾ pound Brussels sprouts
- 1 cup walnuts
- Juice from 1 lemon
- ½ cup grated parmesan cheese
- Salt and pepper to taste

Directions:

1. Heat oil in a skillet over medium flame and sauté the Brussels sprouts for 3 minutes until slightly wilted. Removed from heat and allow to cool.

2. In a bowl, toss together the cooled Brussels sprouts and the rest of the ingredients.

3. Toss to coat.

Nutrition Info:

- Per Servings 8g Carbs, 6g Protein, 23g Fat, 259 Calories

Fruit Salad With Poppy Seeds

Servings: 5
Cooking Time: 25 Mins

Ingredients:

- 1 tablespoon poppy seeds
- 1 head romaine lettuce, torn into bite-size pieces
- 4 ounces shredded Swiss cheese
- 1 avocado- peeled, cored and diced
- 2 teaspoons diced onion
- 1/2 cup lemon juice
- 1/2 cup stevia
- 1/2 teaspoon salt
- 2/3 cup olive oil
- 1 teaspoon Dijon style prepared mustard

Directions:

1. Combine stevia, lemon juice, onion, mustard, and salt in

a blender. Process until well blended.

2. Add oil until mixture is thick and smooth. Add poppy seeds, stir just a few seconds or more to mix.

3. In a large serving bowl, toss together the remaining ingredients.

4. Pour dressing over salad just before serving, and toss to coat.

Nutrition Info:
- Per Servings 6g Carbs, 4.9g Protein, 20.6g Fat, 277 Calories

Balsamic Cucumber Salad

Servings: 6
Cooking Time: 0 Minutes

Ingredients:
- 1 large English cucumber, halved and sliced
- 1 cup grape tomatoes, halved
- 1 medium red onion, sliced thinly
- ¼ cup balsamic vinaigrette
- ¾ cup feta cheese
- Salt and pepper to taste
- ¼ cup olive oil

Directions:
1. Place all ingredients in a bowl.
2. Toss to coat everything with the dressing.
3. Allow chilling before serving.

Nutrition Info:
- Per Servings 9g Carbs, 4.8g Protein, 16.7g Fat, 253 Calories

Asparagus Niçoise Salad

Servings: 4
Cooking Time: 0 Minutes

Ingredients:
- 1-pound fresh asparagus, trimmed and blanched
- 2 ½ ounces white tuna in oil
- ½ cup pitted Greek olives, halved
- ½ cup zesty Italian salad dressing
- Salt and pepper to taste
- 3 tablespoons olive oil

Directions:
1. Place all ingredients in a bowl.
2. Toss to mix all ingredients.
3. Serve.

Nutrition Info:
- Per Servings 10g Carbs, 8g Protein, 20g Fat, 239 Calories

Cobb Egg Salad In Lettuce Cups

Servings: 4
Cooking Time: 20 Minutes

Ingredients:
- 2 chicken breasts, cut into pieces
- 1 tbsp olive oil
- Salt and black pepper to season
- 6 large eggs
- 1 ½ cups water
- 2 tomatoes, seeded, chopped
- 6 tbsp Greek yogurt
- 1 head green lettuce, firm leaves removed for cups

Directions:
1. Preheat oven to 400ºF. Put the chicken pieces in a bowl, drizzle with olive oil, and sprinkle with salt and black pepper. Mix the ingredients until the chicken is well coated with the seasoning.

2. Put the chicken on a prepared baking sheet and spread out evenly. Slide the baking sheet in the oven and bake the chicken until cooked through and golden brown for 8 minutes, turning once.

3. Bring the eggs to boil in salted water in a pot over medium heat for 6 minutes. Run the eggs in cold water, peel, and chop into small pieces. Transfer to a salad bowl.

4. Remove the chicken from the oven when ready and add to the salad bowl. Include the tomatoes and Greek yogurt; mix evenly with a spoon. Layer two lettuce leaves each as cups and fill with two tablespoons of egg salad each. Serve with chilled blueberry juice.

Nutrition Info:
- Per Servings 4g Carbs, 21g Protein, 24.5g Fat, 325 Calories

Mexican Soup

Servings: 4
Cooking Time: 25 Minutes

Ingredients:
- 1-pound boneless skinless chicken thighs, cut into 3/4-inch pieces
- 1 tablespoon reduced-sodium taco seasoning
- 1 cup salsa
- 1 carton reduced-sodium chicken broth
- 4 tablespoons olive oil

Directions:
1. In a large saucepan, heat oil over medium-high heat. Add chicken; cook and stir 6-8 minutes or until no longer pink. Stir in taco seasoning.

2. Add remaining ingredients; bring to a boil. Reduce heat; simmer, uncovered, 5 minutes to allow flavors to blend. Skim fat before serving.

Nutrition Info:

- Per Servings 5.6g Carbs, 25g Protein, 16.5g Fat, 281 Calories

Broccoli Cheese Soup

Servings: 4
Cooking Time: 20 Minutes

Ingredients:
- ¾ cup heavy cream
- 1 onion, diced
- 1 tsp minced garlic
- 4 cups chopped broccoli
- 4 cups veggie broth
- 2 tbsp butter
- 2 ¾ cups grated cheddar cheese
- ¼ cup cheddar cheese to garnish
- Salt and black pepper, to taste
- ½ bunch fresh mint, chopped

Directions:
1. Melt the butter in a large pot over medium heat. Sauté onion and garlic for 3 minutes or until tender, stirring occasionally. Season with salt and pepper. Add the broth, broccoli and bring to a boil.
2. Reduce the heat and simmer for 10 minutes. Puree the soup with a hand blender until smooth. Add in the cheese and cook about 1 minute. Taste, season with salt and pepper. Stir in the heavy cream.Serve in bowls with the reserved grated Cheddar cheese and sprinkled with fresh mint.

Nutrition Info:
- Per Servings 7g Carbs, 23.8g Protein, 52.3g Fat, 561 Calories

Pork Burger Salad With Yellow Cheddar

Servings: 4
Cooking Time: 25 Minutes

Ingredients:
- 1 lb ground pork
- Salt and black pepper to season
- 1 tbsp olive oil
- 2 hearts romaine lettuce, torn into pieces
- 2 firm tomatoes, sliced
- ¼ red onion, sliced
- 3 oz yellow cheddar cheese, shredded

Directions:
1. Season the pork with salt and black pepper, mix and make medium-sized patties out of them.
2. Heat the oil in a skillet over medium heat and fry the patties on both sides for 10 minutes until browned and cook within. Transfer to a wire rack to drain oil. When cooled, cut into quarters.
3. Mix the lettuce, tomatoes, and red onion in a salad bowl,

season with a little oil, salt, and pepper. Toss and add the pork on top.
4. Melt the cheese in the microwave for about 90 seconds. Drizzle the cheese over the salad and serve.

Nutrition Info:
- Per Servings 2g Carbs, 22g Protein, 23g Fat, 310 Calories

Coconut Cauliflower Soup

Servings: 10
Cooking Time: 26 Minutes

Ingredients:
- 1 medium onion, finely chopped
- 3 tablespoons yellow curry paste
- 2 medium heads cauliflower, broken into florets
- 1 carton vegetable broth
- 1 cup coconut milk
- 2 tablespoons olive oil

Directions:
1. In a large saucepan, heat oil over medium heat. Add onion; cook and stir until softened, 2-3 minutes.
2. Add curry paste; cook until fragrant, 1-2 minutes.
3. Add cauliflower and broth. Increase heat to high; bring to a boil. Reduce heat to medium-low; cook, covered, about 20 minutes.
4. Stir in coconut milk; cook an additional minute.
5. Remove from heat; cool slightly.
6. Puree in batches in a blender or food processor.
7. If desired, top with minced fresh cilantro.

Nutrition Info:
- Per Servings 10g Carbs, 3g Protein, 8g Fat, 111 Calories

Rustic Beef Soup

Servings: 4
Cooking Time: 20 Minutes

Ingredients:
- 3 cups beef broth
- 2 cups frozen mixed vegetables
- 1 teaspoon ground mustard
- Beef roast
- 1 teaspoon water
- Pinch of salt

Directions:
1. In a large saucepan, combine all the ingredients.
2. Bring to a boil.
3. Reduce heat; simmer, uncovered, for 15-20 minutes or until barley is tender.

Nutrition Info:
- Per Servings 8g Carbs, 51g Protein, 24g Fat, 450 Calories

Sour Cream And Cucumbers

Servings: 8
Cooking Time: 0 Minutes

Ingredients:
- ½ cup sour cream
- 3 tablespoons white vinegar
- 4 medium cucumbers, sliced thinly
- 1 small sweet onion, sliced thinly
- Salt and pepper to taste
- 3 tablespoons olive oil

Directions:
1. In a bowl, whisk the sour cream and vinegar. Season with salt and pepper to taste. Whisk until well-combined.
2. Add in the cucumber and the rest of the ingredients.
3. Toss to coat.
4. Allow chilling before serving.

Nutrition Info:
- Per Servings 4.8g Carbs, 0.9g Protein, 8.3g Fat, 96 Calories

Caesar Salad With Chicken And Parmesan

Servings: 4
Cooking Time: 1 Hour And 30 Minutes

Ingredients:
- 4 boneless, skinless chicken thighs
- ¼ cup lemon juice
- 2 garlic cloves, minced
- 4 tbsp olive oil
- ½ cup caesar salad dressing, sugar-free
- 12 bok choy leaves
- 3 Parmesan crisps
- Parmesan cheese, grated for garnishing

Directions:
1. Combine the chicken, lemon juice, 2 tbsp of olive oil, and garlic in a Ziploc bag. Seal the bag, shake to combine, and refrigerate for 1 hour. Preheat the grill to medium heat and grill the chicken for about 4 minutes per side.
2. Cut the bok choy leaves lengthwise, and brush it with the remaining olive oil. Grill the bok choy for about 3 minutes. Place on a serving bowl. Top with the chicken and drizzle the caesar salad dressing over. Top with parmesan crisps and sprinkle the grated parmesan cheese over.

Nutrition Info:
- Per Servings 5g Carbs, 33g Protein, 39g Fat, 529 Calories

Spicy Chicken Bean Soup

Servings: 8
Cooking Time:1h 20 Mins

Ingredients:
- 8 skinless, boneless chicken breast halves
- 5 cubes chicken bouillon
- 2 cans peeled and diced tomatoes
- 1 container sour cream
- 1 cups frozen cut green beans
- 3 tablespoons. olive oil
- Salt and black pepper to taste
- 1 onion, chopped
- 3 cloves garlic, chopped
- 1 cups frozen cut green beans

Directions:
1. Heat olive oil in a large pot over medium heat, add onion, garlic and cook until tender. Stir in water, chicken, salt, pepper, bouillon cubes and bring to boil, simmer for 1 hour on Low. Remove chicken from the pot, reserve 5 cups broth and slice.
2. Stir in the remaining ingredients in the pot and simmer 30 minutes. Serve and enjoy.

Nutrition Info:
- Per Servings 7.6g Carbs, 26.5g Protein, 15.3g Fat, 275.1 Calories

Strawberry Salad With Spinach, Cheese & Almonds

Servings: 2
Cooking Time: 20 Minutes

Ingredients:
- 4 cups spinach
- 4 strawberries, sliced
- ½ cup flaked almonds
- 1 ½ cup grated hard goat cheese
- 4 tbsp raspberry vinaigrette
- Salt and black pepper, to taste

Directions:
1. Preheat your oven to 400°F. Arrange the grated goat cheese in two circles on two pieces of parchment paper. Place in the oven and bake for 10 minutes.
2. Find two same bowls, place them upside down, and carefully put the parchment paper on top to give the cheese a bowl-like shape. Let cool that way for 15 minutes. Divide spinach among the bowls stir in salt, pepper and drizzle with vinaigrette. Top with almonds and strawberries.

Nutrition Info:
- Per Servings 5.3g Carbs, 33g Protein, 34.2g Fat, 445 Calories

Creamy Cauliflower Soup With Bacon Chips

Servings: 4
Cooking Time: 25 Minutes

Ingredients:
- 2 tbsp ghee
- 1 onion, chopped
- 2 head cauliflower, cut into florets
- 2 cups water
- Salt and black pepper to taste
- 3 cups almond milk
- 1 cup shredded white cheddar cheese
- 3 bacon strips

Directions:
1. Melt the ghee in a saucepan over medium heat and sauté the onion for 3 minutes until fragrant.
2. Include the cauli florets, sauté for 3 minutes to slightly soften, add the water, and season with salt and black pepper. Bring to a boil, and then reduce the heat to low. Cover and cook for 10 minutes.
3. Puree cauliflower with an immersion blender until the ingredients are evenly combined and stir in the almond milk and cheese until the cheese melts. Adjust taste with salt and black pepper.
4. In a non-stick skillet over high heat, fry the bacon, until crispy. Divide soup between serving bowls, top with crispy bacon, and serve hot.

Nutrition Info:
- Per Servings 6g Carbs, 8g Protein, 37g Fat, 402 Calories

Salsa Verde Chicken Soup

Servings: 4
Cooking Time: 15 Minutes

Ingredients:
- ½ cup salsa verde
- 2 cups cooked and shredded chicken
- 2 cups chicken broth
- 1 cup shredded cheddar cheese
- 4 ounces cream cheese
- ½ tsp chili powder
- ½ tsp ground cumin
- ½ tsp fresh cilantro, chopped
- Salt and black pepper, to taste

Directions:
1. Combine the cream cheese, salsa verde, and broth, in a food processor; pulse until smooth. Transfer the mixture to a pot and place over medium heat. Cook until hot, but do not bring to a boil.
2. Add chicken, chili powder, and cumin and cook for about 3-5 minutes, or until it is heated through.
3. Stir in Cheddar cheese and season with salt and pepper

to taste. If it is very thick, add a few tablespoons of water and boil for 1-3 more minutes. Serve hot in bowls sprinkled with fresh cilantro.

Nutrition Info:
- Per Servings 3g Carbs, 25g Protein, 23g Fat, 346 Calories

Easy Tomato Salad

Servings: 4
Cooking Time: 0 Minutes

Ingredients:
- 1 ½ cups cherry tomatoes, sliced
- ¼ cup white wine vinegar
- 1/8 cup chives
- 3 tablespoons olive oil
- Salt and pepper to taste

Directions:
1. Put all ingredients in a bowl.
2. Toss to combine.
3. Serve immediately.

Nutrition Info:
- Per Servings 0.6g Carbs, 0.3g Protein, 10.1g Fat, 95 Calories

Thyme & Wild Mushroom Soup

Servings: 4
Cooking Time: 25 Minutes

Ingredients:
- ¼ cup butter
- ½ cup crème fraiche
- 12 oz wild mushrooms, chopped
- 2 tsp thyme leaves
- 2 garlic cloves, minced
- 4 cups chicken broth
- Salt and black pepper, to taste

Directions:
1. Melt the butter in a large pot over medium heat. Add garlic and cook for one minute until tender. Add mushrooms, salt and pepper, and cook for 10 minutes. Pour the broth over and bring to a boil.
2. Reduce the heat and simmer for 10 minutes. Puree the soup with a hand blender until smooth. Stir in crème Fraiche. Garnish with thyme leaves before serving.

Nutrition Info:
- Per Servings 5.8g Carbs, 6.1g Protein, 25g Fat, 281 Calories

Arugula Prawn Salad With Mayo Dressing

Servings: 4
Cooking Time: 15 Minutes

Ingredients:

- 4 cups baby arugula
- ½ cup garlic mayonnaise
- 3 tbsp olive oil
- 1 lb tiger prawns, peeled and deveined
- 1 tsp Dijon mustard
- Salt and chili pepper to season
- 2 tbsp lemon juice

Directions:

1. Add the mayonnaise, lemon juice and mustard in a small bowl. Mix until smooth and creamy. Heat 2 tbps of olive oil in a skillet over medium heat, add the prawns, season with salt, and chili pepper, and fry in the oil for 3 minutes on each side until prawns are pink. Set aside to a plate.
2. Place the arugula in a serving bowl and pour half of the dressing on the salad. Toss with 2 spoons until mixed, and add the remaining dressing. Divide salad into 4 plates and serve with prawns.

Nutrition Info:

- Per Servings 2g Carbs, 8g Protein, 20.3g Fat, 215 Calories

Strawberry, Mozzarella Salad

Servings: 3
Cooking Time: 10 Minutes

Ingredients:

- 5 ounces organic salad greens of your choice
- 2 medium cucumber, spiralized
- 2 cups strawberries, hulled and chopped
- 8 ounces mini mozzarella cheese balls
- ½ cup balsamic vinegar
- 5 tablespoons olive oil
- Salt to taste

Directions:

1. Toss all ingredients in a salad bowl.
2. Allow chilling in the fridge for at least 10 minutes before serving.

Nutrition Info:

- Per Servings 10g Carbs, 7g Protein, 31g Fat, 351 Calories

Mediterranean Salad

Servings: 4
Cooking Time: 10 Minutes

Ingredients:

- 3 tomatoes, sliced
- 1 large avocado, sliced
- 8 kalamata olives
- ¼ lb buffalo mozzarella cheese, sliced
- 2 tbsp pesto sauce
- 2 tbsp olive oil

Directions:

1. Arrange the tomato slices on a serving platter and place the avocado slices in the middle. Arrange the olives around the avocado slices and drop pieces of mozzarella on the platter. Drizzle the pesto sauce all over, and drizzle olive oil as well.

Nutrition Info:

- Per Servings 4.3g Carbs, 9g Protein, 25g Fat, 290 Calories

Pork, Beef & Lamb Recipes

Pork, Beef & Lamb Recipes

Pork Casserole

Servings: 4
Cooking Time: 38 Minutes

Ingredients:
- 1 lb ground pork
- 1 large yellow squash, thinly sliced
- Salt and black pepper to taste
- 1 clove garlic, minced
- 4 green onions, chopped
- 1 cup chopped cremini mushrooms
- 1 can diced tomatoes
- ½ cup pork rinds, crushed
- ¼ cup chopped parsley
- 1 cup cottage cheese
- 1 cup Mexican cheese blend
- 3 tbsp olive oil
- ⅓ cup water

Directions:
1. Preheat the oven to 370ºF.
2. Heat the olive oil in a skillet over medium heat, add the pork, season it with salt and pepper, and cook for 3 minutes or until no longer pink. Stir occasionally while breaking any lumps apart.
3. Add the garlic, half of the green onions, mushrooms, and 2 tablespoons of pork rinds. Continue cooking for 3 minutes. Stir in the tomatoes, half of the parsley, and water. Cook further for 3 minutes, and then turn the heat off.
4. Mix the remaining parsley, cottage cheese, and Mexican cheese blend. Set aside. Sprinkle the bottom of a baking dish with 3 tablespoons of pork rinds; top with half of the squash and a season of salt, 2/3 of the pork mixture, and the cheese mixture. Repeat the layering process a second time to exhaust the ingredients.
5. Cover the baking dish with foil and put in the oven to bake for 20 minutes. After, remove the foil and brown the top of the casserole with the broiler side of the oven for 2 minutes. Remove the dish when ready and serve the casserole warm.

Nutrition Info:
- Per Servings 2.7g Carbs, 36.5g Protein, 29g Fat, 495 Calories

Jamaican Pork Oven Roast

Servings: 12
Cooking Time: 4 Hours And 20 Minutes

Ingredients:
- 4 pounds pork roast
- 1 tbsp olive oil
- ¼ cup jerk spice blend
- ½ cup vegetable stock
- Salt and ground pepper, to taste

Directions:
1. Rub the pork with olive oil and the spice blend. Heat a dutch oven over medium heat and sear the meat well on all sides; add in the stock. Cover the pot, reduce the heat, and let cook for 4 hours.

Nutrition Info:
- Per Servings 0g Carbs, 23g Protein, 24g Fat, 282 Calories

Beef Italian Sandwiches

Servings: 6
Cooking Time: 40 Minutes

Ingredients:
- 6 Provolone cheese slices
- 14.5-ounce can beef broth
- 8-ounces giardiniera drained (Chicago-style Italian sandwich mix)
- 3-pounds chuck roast fat trimmed and cut into large pieces
- 6 large lettuce
- Pepper and salt to taste

Directions:
1. Add all ingredients in a pot, except for lettuce and cheese, on high fire, and bring to a boil.
2. Once boiling, lower fire to a simmer and cook for 25 minutes.
3. Adjust seasoning to taste.
4. To make a sandwich, add warm shredded beef in one lettuce leaf and top with cheese.

Nutrition Info:
- Per Servings 3.9g Carbs, 48.6g Protein, 36.4g Fat, 538 Calories

Rack Of Lamb In Red Bell Pepper Butter Sauce

Servings: 4
Cooking Time: 65 Minutes + Cooling Time

Ingredients:
- 1 lb rack of lamb
- Salt to cure
- 3 cloves garlic, minced
- ⅓ cup olive oil
- ⅓ cup white wine
- 6 sprigs fresh rosemary
- Water for soaking
- Sauce
- 2 tbsp olive oil
- 1 large red bell pepper, seeded, diced
- 2 cloves garlic, minced
- 1 cup chicken broth
- 2 oz butter
- Salt and white pepper to taste

Directions:
1. Fill a large bowl with water and soak in the lamb for 30 minutes. Drain the meat after and season with salt. Let the lamb sit on a rack to drain completely and then rinse it afterward. Put in a bowl.
2. Mix the olive oil with wine and garlic, and brush the mixture all over the lamb. Drop the rosemary sprigs on it, cover the bowl with plastic wrap, and place in the refrigerator to marinate the meat.
3. The next day, preheat the grill to 450°F and cook the lamb for 6 minutes on both sides. Remove after and let rest for 4 minutes.
4. Heat the olive oil in a frying pan and sauté the garlic and bell pepper for 5 minutes. Pour in the chicken broth and continue cooking the ingredients until the liquid reduces by half, about 10 minutes. Add the butter, salt, and pepper. Stir to melt the butter and turn the heat off.
5. Use the stick blender to puree the ingredients until very smooth and strain the sauce through a fine mesh into a bowl. Slice the lamb, serve with the sauce, and your favorite red wine.

Nutrition Info:
- Per Servings 2g Carbs, 46g Protein, 25g Fat, 415 Calories

Beef Cauliflower Curry

Servings: 6
Cooking Time: 26 Minutes

Ingredients:
- 1 tbsp olive oil
- 1 ½ lb ground beef
- 1 tbsp ginger-garlic paste
- 1 tsp garam masala
- 1 can whole tomatoes
- 1 head cauliflower, cut into florets
- Pink salt and chili pepper to taste
- ¼ cup water

Directions:
1. Heat oil in a saucepan over medium heat, add the beef, ginger-garlic paste and season with garam masala. Cook for 5 minutes while breaking any lumps.
2. Stir in the tomatoes and cauliflower, season with salt and chili pepper, and cook covered for 6 minutes. Add the water and bring to a boil over medium heat for 10 minutes or until the water has reduced by half. Adjust taste with salt.
3. Spoon the curry into serving bowls and serve with shirataki rice.

Nutrition Info:
- Per Servings 2g Carbs, 22g Protein, 33g Fat, 374 Calories

Beef And Egg Rice Bowls

Servings: 4
Cooking Time: 22 Minutes

Ingredients:
- 2 cups cauli rice
- 3 cups frozen mixed vegetables
- 3 tbsp ghee
- 1 lb skirt steak
- Salt and black pepper to taste
- 4 fresh eggs
- Hot sauce (sugar-free) for topping

Directions:
1. Mix the cauli rice and mixed vegetables in a bowl, sprinkle with a little water, and steam in the microwave for 1 minute to be tender. Share into 4 serving bowls.
2. Melt the ghee in a skillet, season the beef with salt and pepper, and brown for 5 minutes on each side. Use a perforated spoon to ladle the meat onto the vegetables.
3. Wipe out the skillet and return to medium heat, crack in an egg, season with salt and pepper and cook until the egg white has set, but the yolk is still runny 3 minutes. Remove egg onto the vegetable bowl and fry the remaining 3 eggs. Add to the other bowls.
4. Drizzle the beef bowls with hot sauce and serve.

Nutrition Info:
- Per Servings 4g Carbs, 15g Protein, 26g Fat, 320 Calories

Beef Zucchini Boats

Servings: 4
Cooking Time: 45 Minutes

Ingredients:
- 2 garlic cloves, minced
- 1 tsp cumin
- 1 tbsp olive oil
- 1 pound ground beef
- ½ cup onion, chopped
- 1 tsp smoked paprika
- Salt and ground black pepper, to taste
- 4 zucchinis
- ¼ cup fresh cilantro, chopped
- ½ cup Monterey Jack cheese, shredded
- 1½ cups enchilada sauce
- 1 avocado, chopped, for serving
- Green onions, chopped, for serving
- Tomatoes, chopped, for serving

Directions:
1. Set a pan over high heat and warm the oil. Add the onions, and cook for 2 minutes. Stir in the beef, and brown for 4-5 minutes. Stir in the paprika, pepper, garlic, cumin, and salt; cook for 2 minutes.
2. Slice the zucchini in half lengthwise and scoop out the seeds. Set the zucchini in a greased baking pan, stuff each with the beef, scatter enchilada sauce on top, and spread with the Monterey cheese.
3. Bake in the oven at 350ºF for 20 minutes while covered. Uncover, spread with cilantro, and bake for 5 minutes. Top with tomatoes, green onions and avocado, place on serving plates and enjoy.

Nutrition Info:
- Per Servings 7.8g Carbs, 39g Protein, 33g Fat, 422 Calories

Greek Pork With Olives

Servings: 4
Cooking Time: 45 Minutes

Ingredients:
- 4 pork chops, bone-in
- Salt and ground black pepper, to taste
- 1 tsp dried rosemary
- 3 garlic cloves, peeled and minced
- ½ cup kalamata olives, pitted and sliced
- 2 tbsp olive oil
- ¼ cup vegetable broth

Directions:
1. Season pork chops with pepper and salt, and add in a roasting pan. Stir in the garlic, olives, olive oil, broth, and rosemary, set in the oven at 425ºF, and bake for 10 minutes. Reduce heat to 350ºF and roast for 25 minutes. Slice the pork, split among plates, and sprinkle with pan juices all over.

Nutrition Info:
- Per Servings 2.2g Carbs, 36g Protein, 25.2g Fat, 415 Calories

Beef Stew With Bacon

Servings: 6
Cooking Time: 1 Hour 15 Minutes

Ingredients:
- 8 ounces bacon, chopped
- 4 lb beef meat for stew, cubed
- 4 garlic cloves, minced
- 2 brown onions, chopped
- 2 tbsp olive oil
- 4 tbsp red vinegar
- 4 cups beef stock
- 2 tbsp tomato puree
- 2 cinnamon sticks
- 3 lemon peel strips
- ½ cup fresh parsley, chopped
- 4 thyme sprigs
- 2 tbsp butter
- Salt and black pepper, to taste

Directions:
1. Set a saucepan over medium-high heat and warm oil, add in the garlic, bacon, and onion, and cook for 5 minutes. Stir in the beef, and cook until slightly brown. Pour in the vinegar, pepper, butter, lemon peel strips, stock, salt, tomato puree, cinnamon sticks and thyme; stir for 3 minutes.
2. Cook for 1 hour while covered. Get rid of the thyme, lemon peel, and cinnamon sticks. Split into serving bowls and sprinkle with parsley to serve.

Nutrition Info:
- Per Servings 5.7g Carbs, 63g Protein, 36g Fat, 592 Calories

Dr. Pepper Pulled Pork

Servings: 9
Cooking Time: 45 Minutes

Ingredients:
- 3 pounds pork loin roast, chopped into 8 equal pieces
- 1 packet pork rub seasoning
- 1 12-ounce can Dr. Pepper
- ½ cup commercial BBQ sauce
- 1 bay leaf
- 1 tsp oil
- 2 tbsp water

Directions:
1. Place a heavy-bottomed pot on medium-high fire and heat for 2 minutes. Add oil and swirl to coat the bottom and

sides of pot and heat for a minute.

2. Brown roast for 4 minutes per side.

3. Add remaining ingredients.

4. Cover and simmer for 30 minutes or until pork is fork-tender. Stir the bottom of the pot every now and then. Turn off the fire.

5. With two forks, shred pork.

6. Turn on fire to high and boil uncovered until sauce is rendered, around 5 minutes.

7. Serve and enjoy.

Nutrition Info:
• Per Servings 4.6g Carbs, 40.9g Protein, 13.4g Fat, 310 Calories

Pork Medallion With Herbes De Provence

Servings: 2
Cooking Time: 15 Minutes

Ingredients:
• 8 ounces of pork medallion, trimmed from fat
• ½ teaspoon Herbes de Provence
• ¼ cup dry white wine
• Freshly ground black pepper to taste
• Salt to taste

Directions:
1. Season the meat with black pepper.
2. Place the meat in between sheets of wax paper and pound on a mallet until about ¼ inch thick.
3. In a nonstick skillet, sear the pork over medium heat for 5 minutes on each side or until the meat is slightly brown.
4. Remove meat from the skillet and sprinkle with herbes de Provence.
5. Using the same skillet, pour the wine and scrape the sides to deglaze. Allow simmering until the wine is reduced.
6. Pour the wine sauce over the pork.
7. Serve immediately.

Nutrition Info:
• Per Servings 1.0g Carbs, 24.0g Protein, 24.0g Fat, 316 Calories

Stuffed Pork With Red Cabbage Salad

Servings: 4
Cooking Time: 40 Minutes

Ingredients:
• Zest and juice from 2 limes
• 2 garlic cloves, minced
• ¾ cup olive oil
• 1 cup fresh cilantro, chopped
• 1 cup fresh mint, chopped
• 1 tsp dried oregano
• Salt and black pepper, to taste
• 2 tsp cumin
• 4 pork loin steaks
• 2 pickles, chopped
• 4 ham slices
• 6 Swiss cheese slices
• 2 tbsp mustard
• For the Salad
• 1 head red cabbage, shredded
• 2 tbsp vinegar
• 3 tbsp olive oil
• Salt to taste

Directions:
1. In a food processor, combine the lime zest, oil, oregano, pepper, cumin, cilantro, lime juice, garlic, mint, and salt. Season the steaks with pepper and salt, set them into a bowl, place in the marinade, and toss well to coat; set aside for some hours in the fridge.
2. Arrange the steaks on a working surface, split the pickles, mustard, cheese, and ham on them, roll, and secure with toothpicks. Heat a pan over medium heat, add in the pork rolls, cook each side for 2 minutes and remove to a baking sheet. Bake in the oven at 350°F for 25 minutes. Meanwhile, prepare the red cabbage salad by mixing all salad ingredients and serve with the meat.

Nutrition Info:
• Per Servings 3g Carbs, 26g Protein, 37g Fat, 413 Calories

Bbq Pork Pizza With Goat Cheese

Servings: 4
Cooking Time: 30 Minutes

Ingredients:
• 1 low carb pizza bread
• Olive oil for brushing
• 1 cup grated manchego cheese
• 2 cups leftover pulled pork
• ½ cup sugar-free BBQ sauce
• 1 cup crumbled goat cheese

Directions:
1. Preheat oven to 400°F and put pizza bread on a pizza pan. Brush with olive oil and sprinkle the manchego cheese all over. Mix the pork with BBQ sauce and spread over the cheese. Drop goat cheese on top and bake for 25 minutes until the cheese has melted and golden brown on top. Slice the pizza with a cutter and serve warm.

Nutrition Info:
• Per Servings 6g Carbs, 5g Protein, 24g Fat, 344 Calories

Beef Cotija Cheeseburger

Servings: 4
Cooking Time: 15 Minutes

Ingredients:
- 1 lb ground beef
- 1 tsp dried parsley
- ½ tsp sugar-free Worcestershire sauce
- Salt and black pepper to taste
- 1 cup cotija cheese, shredded
- 4 low carb buns, halved

Directions:
1. Preheat a grill to 400ºF and grease the grate with cooking spray.
2. Mix the beef, parsley, Worcestershire sauce, salt, and black pepper with your hands until evenly combined. Make medium sized patties out of the mixture, about 4 patties. Cook on the grill for 7 minutes one side to be cooked through and no longer pink.
3. Flip the patties and top with cheese. Cook for another 7 minutes to be well done while the cheese melts onto the meat. Remove the patties and sandwich into two halves of a bun each. Serve with a tomato dipping sauce and zucchini fries.

Nutrition Info:
- Per Servings 2g Carbs, 21g Protein, 32g Fat, 386 Calories

Pork And Mushroom Bake

Servings: 6
Cooking Time: 1 Hour And 15 Minutes

Ingredients:
- 1 onion, chopped
- 2 cans mushroom soup
- 6 pork chops
- ½ cup sliced mushrooms
- Salt and ground pepper, to taste

Directions:
1. Preheat the oven to 370ºF.
2. Season the pork chops with salt and pepper, and place in a baking dish. Combine the mushroom soup, mushrooms, and onion, in a bowl. Pour this mixture over the pork chops. Bake for 45 minutes.

Nutrition Info:
- Per Servings 8g Carbs, 19.4g Protein, 32.6g Fat, 403 Calories

Beef And Ale Pot Roast

Servings: 6
Cooking Time: 2 Hours 20 Minutes

Ingredients:
- 1 ½ lb brisket
- 1 tbsp olive oil
- 8 baby carrots, peeled
- 2 medium red onions, quartered
- 4 stalks celery, cut into chunks
- Salt and black pepper to taste
- 2 bay leaves
- 1 ½ cups low carb beer (ale)

Directions:
1. Preheat the oven to 370ºF. Heat the olive oil in a large skillet, while heating, season the brisket with salt and pepper. Brown the meat on both sides for 8 minutes. After, transfer to a deep casserole dish.
2. In the dish, arrange the carrots, onions, celery, and bay leaves around the brisket and pour the beer all over it. Cover the pot and cook the ingredients in the oven for 2 hours.
3. When ready, remove the casserole. Transfer the beef to a chopping board and cut it into thick slices. Serve the beef and vegetables with a drizzle of the sauce and with steamed turnips.

Nutrition Info:
- Per Servings 6g Carbs, 26g Protein, 34g Fat, 513 Calories

Juicy Pork Medallions

Servings: 4
Cooking Time: 55 Minutes

Ingredients:
- 2 onions, chopped
- 6 bacon slices, chopped
- ½ cup vegetable stock
- Salt and black pepper, to taste
- 1 pound pork tenderloin, cut into medallions

Directions:
1. Set a pan over medium heat, stir in the bacon, cook until crispy, and remove to a plate. Add onions, some pepper, and salt, and cook for 5 minutes; set to the same plate with bacon.
2. Add the pork medallions to the pan, season with pepper and salt, brown for 3 minutes on each side, turn, reduce heat to medium, and cook for 7 minutes. Stir in the stock, and cook for 2 minutes. Return the bacon and onions to the pan and cook for 1 minute.

Nutrition Info:
- Per Servings 6g Carbs, 36g Protein, 18g Fat, 325 Calories

Homemade Classic Beef Burgers

Servings: 4
Cooking Time: 15 Minutes

Ingredients:
- 1 pound ground beef
- ½ tsp onion powder
- ½ tsp garlic powder
- 2 tbsp ghee
- 1 tsp Dijon mustard
- 4 low carb buns, halved
- ¼ cup mayonnaise
- 1 tsp sriracha
- 4 tbsp cabbage slaw

Directions:
1. Mix together the beef, onion, garlic powder, mustard, salt, and black pepper; create 4 burgers. Melt the ghee in a skillet and cook the burgers for about 3 minutes per side. Serve in buns topped with mayo, sriracha, and slaw.

Nutrition Info:
- Per Servings 7.9g Carbs, 39g Protein, 55g Fat, 664 Calories

Pork Pie With Cauliflower

Servings: 8
Cooking Time: 1 Hour And 30 Minutes

Ingredients:
- Crust:
- 1 egg
- ¼ cup butter
- 2 cups almond flour
- ¼ tsp xanthan gum
- ¼ cup shredded mozzarella
- A pinch of salt
- Filling:
- 2 pounds ground pork
- ½ cup water
- ⅓ cup pureed onion
- ¾ tsp allspice
- 1 cup cooked and mashed cauliflower
- 1 tbsp ground sage
- 2 tbsp butter

Directions:
1. Preheat your oven to 350ºF.
2. Whisk together all crust ingredients in a bowl. Make two balls out of the mixture and refrigerate for 10 minutes. Combine the water, meat, and salt, in a pot over medium heat. Cook for about 15 minutes, place the meat along with the other ingredients in a bowl. Mix with your hands to combine.
3. Roll out the pie crusts and place one at the bottom of a greased pie pan. Spread the filling over the crust. Top with

the other coat. Bake in the oven for 50 minutes then serve.

Nutrition Info:
- Per Servings 4g Carbs, 29g Protein, 41g Fat, 485 Calories

Meatballs With Ranch-buffalo Sauce

Servings: 10
Cooking Time: 30 Minutes

Ingredients:
- 1 packet Ranch dressing dry mix
- 1 bottle red-hot wings buffalo sauce
- 1 bag frozen Rosina Italian Style Meatballs
- 5 tablespoons butter
- 1 cup water
- Pepper and salt to taste

Directions:
1. Add all ingredients in a pot on high fire and bring to a boil.
2. Once boiling, lower fire to a simmer and cook for 25 minutes.
3. Adjust seasoning to taste.
4. Serve and enjoy.

Nutrition Info:
- Per Servings 1.2g Carbs, 36.0g Protein, 27.9g Fat, 400 Calories

Pork Sausage With Spinach

Servings: 6
Cooking Time: 35 Minutes

Ingredients:
- 1 onion, chopped
- 2 tbsp olive oil
- 1½ pound Italian pork sausage, sliced
- 1 red bell pepper, seeded and chopped
- Salt and black pepper, to taste
- 4 pounds spinach, chopped
- 1 garlic, minced
- ¼ cup green chili pepper, chopped
- 1 cup water

Directions:
1. Set a pan over medium-high heat, warm oil and cook the sausage for 10 minutes. Stir in the onion, garlic and bell pepper, and fry for 3-4 minutes. Place in the spinach, salt, water, black pepper, chili pepper, and cook for 10 minutes. Split among serving bowls and enjoy.

Nutrition Info:
- Per Servings 6.2g Carbs, 29g Protein, 28g Fat, 352 Calories

Italian Beef Ragout

Servings: 4
Cooking Time: 1 Hour 52 Minutes

Ingredients:
- 1 lb chuck steak, trimmed and cubed
- 2 tbsp olive oil
- Salt and black pepper to taste
- 2 tbsp almond flour
- 1 medium onion, diced
- ½ cup dry white wine
- 1 red bell pepper, seeded and diced
- 2 tsp sugar-free Worcestershire sauce
- 4 oz tomato puree
- 3 tsp smoked paprika
- 1 cup beef broth
- Thyme leaves to garnish

Directions:
1. First, lightly dredge the meat in the almond flour and set aside. Place a large skillet over medium heat, add 1 tablespoon of oil to heat and then sauté the onion, and bell pepper for 3 minutes. Stir in the paprika, and add the remaining olive oil.
2. Add the beef and cook for 10 minutes in total while turning them halfway. Stir in white wine, let it reduce by half, about 3 minutes, and add Worcestershire sauce, tomato puree, and beef broth.
3. Let the mixture boil for 2 minutes, then reduce the heat to lowest and let simmer for 1 ½ hours; stirring now and then. Adjust the taste and dish the ragout. Serve garnished with thyme leaves.

Nutrition Info:
- Per Servings 4.2g Carbs, 36.6g Protein, 21.6g Fat, 328 Calories

Soy-glazed Meatloaf

Servings: 6
Cooking Time: 60 Minutes

Ingredients:
- 1 cup white mushrooms, chopped
- 2 pounds ground beef
- 2 tbsp fresh parsley, chopped
- 2 garlic cloves, minced
- 1 onion, chopped
- 1 red bell pepper, seeded and chopped
- ½ cup almond flour
- ⅓ cup Parmesan cheese, grated
- 2 eggs
- Salt and black pepper, to taste
- 1 tsp balsamic vinegar
- 1 tbsp swerve
- 1 tbsp soy sauce
- 2 tbsp sugar-free ketchup
- 2 cups balsamic vinegar

Directions:
1. Using a bowl, combine the beef with salt, mushrooms, bell pepper, Parmesan cheese, 1 teaspoon vinegar, parsley, garlic, pepper, onion, almond flour, salt, and eggs. Set this into a loaf pan, and bake for 30 minutes in the oven at 370ºF.
2. Meanwhile, heat a small pan over medium heat, add in the 2 cups vinegar, swerve, soy sauce, and ketchup, and cook for 20 minutes. Remove the meatloaf from the oven, spread the glaze over the meatloaf, and bake in the oven for 20 more minutes. Allow the meatloaf to cool, slice, and enjoy.

Nutrition Info:
- Per Servings 7.5g Carbs, 46g Protein, 21.4g Fat, 474 Calories

Balsamic Grilled Pork Chops

Servings: 6
Cooking Time: 2 Hours 20 Minutes

Ingredients:
- 6 pork loin chops, boneless
- 2 tbsp erythritol
- ¼ cup balsamic vinegar
- 3 cloves garlic, minced
- ¼ cup olive oil
- ⅓ tsp salt
- Black pepper to taste

Directions:
1. Put the pork in a plastic bag. In a bowl, mix the erythritol, balsamic vinegar, garlic, olive oil, salt, pepper, and pour the sauce over the pork. Seal the bag, shake it, and place in the refrigerator.
2. Marinate the pork for 1 to 2 hours. Preheat the grill on medium-high heat, remove the pork when ready, and grill covered for 10 to 12 minutes on each side. Remove the pork chops, let them sit for 4 minutes, and serve with a syrupy parsnip sauté.

Nutrition Info:
- Per Servings 1.5g Carbs, 38.1g Protein, 26.8g Fat, 418 Calories

Beef Bourguignon

Servings: 4
Cooking Time: 60 Minutes + Marinated Time

Ingredients:

- 3 tbsp coconut oil
- 1 tbsp dried parsley flakes
- 1 cup red wine
- 1 tsp dried thyme
- Salt and black pepper, to taste
- 1 bay leaf
- ⅓ cup coconut flour
- 2 lb beef, cubed
- 12 small white onions
- 4 pancetta slices, chopped
- 2 garlic cloves, minced
- ½ lb mushrooms, chopped

Directions:

1. In a bowl, combine the wine with bay leaf, olive oil, thyme, pepper, parsley, salt, and the beef cubes; set aside for 3 hours. Drain the meat, and reserve the marinade. Toss the flour over the meat to coat.
2. Heat a pan over medium-high heat, stir in the pancetta, and cook until slightly browned. Place in the onions and garlic, and cook for 3 minutes. Stir-fry in the meat and mushrooms for 4-5 minutes.
3. Pour in the marinade and 1 cup of water; cover and cook for 50 minutes. Season to taste and serve.

Nutrition Info:

- Per Servings 7g Carbs, 45g Protein, 26g Fat, 435 Calories

Garlic Lime Marinated Pork Chops

Servings: 4
Cooking Time: 10 Minutes

Ingredients:

- 4 6-ounce lean boneless pork chops, trimmed from fat
- 4 cloves of garlic, crushed
- 1 teaspoon cumin
- 1 teaspoon paprika
- ½ lime, juiced and zested
- 1 tsp black pepper
- ½ tsp salt
- 5 tablespoons olive oil

Directions:

1. In a bowl, season the pork with the rest of the ingredients.
2. Allow marinating inside the fridge for at least 2 hours.
3. Place the pork chops in a baking dish or broiler pan and grill for 5 minutes on each side until golden brown.
4. Serve with salad if desired.

Nutrition Info:

- Per Servings 2.4g Carbs, 38.5g Protein, 22.9g Fat, 376 Calories

Cranberry Gravy Brisket

Servings: 7
Cooking Time: 25 Minutes

Ingredients:

- 1 tablespoon prepared mustard
- ½ cup chopped onion
- 1 can tomato sauce
- ½ cup cranberries, pitted
- 1 fresh beef brisket
- 5 tablespoons olive oil
- ½ teaspoon salt
- ¼ teaspoon pepper

Directions:

1. Add all ingredients in a pot on high fire and bring to a boil.
2. Once boiling, lower fire to a simmer and cook for 25 minutes.
3. Adjust seasoning to taste.
4. Serve and enjoy.

Nutrition Info:

- Per Servings 9.7g Carbs, 24.9g Protein, 24.4g Fat, 364 Calories

Simple Corned Beef

Servings: 6
Cooking Time: 1 Hour And 30 Minutes

Ingredients:

- 2 pounds corned beef brisket, cut into 1-inch cubes
- 2 cups water
- 2 onions, chopped
- 6 garlic cloves, smashed
- 1 cup olive oil
- 1 tbsp peppercorns
- 1 tsp salt

Directions:

1. Place all ingredients in a heavy-bottomed pot on high fire and bring to a boil.
2. Once boiling, lower fire to a simmer.
3. Simmer for 60 minutes.
4. Turn off fire and shred beef with two forks.
5. Turn on fire and continue cooking until sauce is reduced.
6. Serve and enjoy.

Nutrition Info:

- Per Servings 0.6g Carbs, 12.1g Protein, 30.2g Fat, 314 Calories

Beef And Butternut Squash Stew

Servings: 4
Cooking Time: 40 Minutes

Ingredients:
- 3 tsp olive oil
- 1 pound ground beef
- 1 cup beef stock
- 14 ounces canned tomatoes with juice
- 1 tbsp stevia
- 1 pound butternut squash, chopped
- 1 tbsp Worcestershire sauce
- 2 bay leaves
- Salt and ground black pepper, to taste
- 3 tbsp fresh parsley, chopped
- 1 onion, chopped
- 1 tsp dried sage
- 1 tbsp garlic, minced

Directions:
1. Set a pan over medium heat and heat olive oil, stir in the onion, garlic, and beef, and cook for 10 minutes. Add in butternut squash, Worcestershire sauce, bay leaves, stevia, beef stock, canned tomatoes, and sage, and bring to a boil. Reduce heat, and simmer for 20 minutes.
2. Adjust the seasonings. Split into bowls and enjoy.

Nutrition Info:
- Per Servings 7.3g Carbs, 32g Protein, 17g Fat, 343 Calories

Sweet Chipotle Grilled Ribs

Servings: 4
Cooking Time: 32 Minutes

Ingredients:
- 2 tbsp erythritol
- Pink salt and black pepper to taste
- 1 tbsp olive oil
- 3 tsp chipotle powder
- 1 tsp garlic powder
- 1 lb spare ribs
- 4 tbsp sugar-free BBQ sauce + extra for serving

Directions:
1. Mix the erythritol, salt, pepper, oil, chipotle, and garlic powder. Brush on the meaty sides of the ribs and wrap in foil. Sit for 30 minutes to marinate.
2. Preheat oven to 400ºF, place wrapped ribs on a baking sheet, and cook for 40 minutes to be cooked through. Remove ribs and aluminium foil, brush with BBQ sauce, and brown under the broiler for 10 minutes on both sides. Slice and serve with extra BBQ sauce and lettuce tomato salad.

Nutrition Info:
- Per Servings 3g Carbs, 21g Protein, 33g Fat, 395 Calories

Veal Stew

Servings: 6
Cooking Time: 2 Hours

Ingredients:
- 2 tbsp olive oil
- 3 pounds veal shoulder, cubed
- 1 onion, chopped
- 1 garlic clove, minced
- Salt and black pepper, to taste
- 1 cup water
- 1 ½ cups red wine
- 12 ounces canned tomato sauce
- 1 carrot, chopped
- 1 cup mushrooms, chopped
- ½ cup green beans
- 2 tsp dried oregano

Directions:
1. Set a pot over medium-high heat and warm the oil. Brown the veal for 5-6 minutes. Stir in the onion, and garlic, and cook for 3 minutes. Place in the wine, oregano, carrots, pepper, salt, tomato sauce, water, and mushrooms, bring to a boil, reduce the heat to low.
2. Cook for 1 hour and 45 minutes, then in the green beans and cook for 5 minutes. Season with more black pepper and salt, split among serving bowls to serve.

Nutrition Info:
- Per Servings 5.2g Carbs, 44g Protein, 21g Fat, 415 Calories

Poultry Recipes

Poultry Recipes

Stir Fried Broccoli 'n Chicken

Servings: 5
Cooking Time: 20 Minutes

Ingredients:
- 1 tbsp. coconut oil
- 3 cloves of garlic, minced
- 1 ½ lb. chicken breasts, cut into strips
- ¼ cup coconut aminos
- 1 head broccoli, cut into florets
- Pepper to taste

Directions:
1. On medium fire, heat a saucepan for 2 minutes. Add oil to the pan and swirl to coat bottom and sides. Heat oil for a minute.
2. Add garlic and sauté for a minute. Stir in chicken and stir fry for 5 minutes.
3. Add remaining ingredients. Season generously with pepper.
4. Increase fire to high and stir fry for 3 minutes.
5. Lower fire to low, cover, and cook for 5 minutes.
6. Serve and enjoy.

Nutrition Info:
- Per Servings 1.8g Carbs, 28.6g Protein, 15.4g Fat, 263 Calories

Quattro Formaggi Chicken

Servings: 8
Cooking Time: 40 Minutes

Ingredients:
- 3 pounds chicken breasts
- 2 ounces mozzarella cheese, cubed
- 2 ounces mascarpone cheese
- 4 ounces cheddar cheese, cubed
- 2 ounces provolone cheese, cubed
- 1 zucchini, shredded
- Salt and ground black pepper, to taste
- 1 tsp garlic, minced
- ½ cup pancetta, cooked and crumbled

Directions:
1. Sprinkle pepper and salt to the zucchini, squeeze well, and place to a bowl. Stir in the pancetta, mascarpone, cheddar cheese, provolone cheese, mozzarella, pepper, and garlic.
2. Cut slits into chicken breasts, apply pepper and salt, and stuff with the zucchini and cheese mixture. Set on a lined baking sheet, place in the oven at 400ºF, and bake for 45 minutes.

Nutrition Info:
- Per Servings 2g Carbs, 51g Protein, 37g Fat, 565 Calories

Creamy Stuffed Chicken With Parma Ham

Servings: 4
Cooking Time: 40 Minutes

Ingredients:
- 4 chicken breasts
- 2 tbsp olive oil
- 3 cloves garlic, minced
- 3 shallots, finely chopped
- 4 tbsp dried mixed herbs
- 8 slices Parma ham
- 8 oz cream cheese
- 2 lemons, zested
- Salt and black pepper to taste

Directions:
1. Preheat the oven to 350ºF.
2. Heat the oil in a small skillet and sauté the garlic and shallots with a pinch of salt and lemon zest for 3 minutes. Turn the heat off and let it cool. After, stir the cream cheese and mixed herbs into the shallot mixture.
3. Score a pocket in each chicken breast, fill the holes with the cream cheese mixture and cover with the cut-out chicken. Wrap each breast with two Parma ham and secure the ends with a toothpick.
4. Lay the chicken parcels on a greased baking sheet and cook in the oven for 20 minutes. After cooking, remove to rest for 4 minutes before serving with a green salad and roasted tomatoes.

Nutrition Info:
- Per Servings 2g Carbs, 26g Protein, 35g Fat, 485 Calories

Rosemary Grilled Chicken

Servings: 4
Cooking Time: 12 Minutes

Ingredients:
- 1 tablespoon fresh parsley, finely chopped
- 1 tablespoon fresh rosemary, finely chopped
- 4 tablespoons olive oil
- 4 pieces of 4-oz chicken breast, boneless and skinless
- 5 cloves garlic, minced
- Pepper and salt to taste

Directions:
1. In a shallow and large bowl, mix salt, parsley, rosemary, olive oil, and garlic. Place chicken breast and marinate in the bowl of herbs for at least an hour or more before grilling.
2. Grease grill, grate and preheat grill to medium-high fire. Once hot, grill chicken for 4 to 5 minutes per side or until juices run a clear and internal temperature of chicken is 168oF.

Nutrition Info:
- Per Servings 1.0g Carbs, 34.0g Protein, 16.0g Fat, 238 Calories

Chicken In Creamy Tomato Sauce

Servings: 6
Cooking Time: 20 Minutes

Ingredients:
- 2 tbsp butter
- 6 chicken thighs
- Pink salt and black pepper to taste
- 14 oz canned tomato sauce
- 2 tsp Italian seasoning
- ½ cup heavy cream
- 1 cup shredded Parmesan cheese
- Parmesan cheese to garnish.

Directions:
1. In a saucepan, melt the butter over medium heat, season the chicken with salt and black pepper, and cook for 5 minutes on each side to brown. Plate the chicken.
2. Pour the tomato sauce and Italian seasoning in the pan and cook covered for 8 minutes. Adjust the taste with salt and black pepper and stir in the heavy cream and Parmesan cheese.
3. Once the cheese has melted, return the chicken to the pot, and simmer for 4 minutes, making sure to coat the chicken with the sauce while cooking.
4. Dish the chicken with sauce, garnish with more Parmesan cheese, and serve with zoodles.

Nutrition Info:
- Per Servings 2g Carbs, 24g Protein, 38.2g Fat, 456 Calories

Cheddar Chicken Tenders

Servings: 4
Cooking Time: 40 Minutes

Ingredients:
- 2 eggs
- 3 tbsp butter, melted
- 3 cups coarsely crushed cheddar cheese
- ½ cup pork rinds, crushed
- 1 lb chicken tenders
- Pink salt to taste

Directions:
1. Preheat oven to 350ºF and line a baking sheet with parchment paper. Whisk the eggs with the butter in one bowl and mix the cheese and pork rinds in another bowl.
2. Season chicken with salt, dip in egg mixture, and coat generously in cheddar mixture. Place on baking sheet, cover with aluminium foil and bake for 25 minutes. Remove foil and bake further for 12 minutes to golden brown. Serve chicken with mustard dip.

Nutrition Info:
- Per Servings 1.3g Carbs, 42g Protein, 54g Fat, 507 Calories

Zucchini Spaghetti With Turkey Bolognese Sauce

Servings: 6
Cooking Time: 30 Minutes

Ingredients:
- 2 cups sliced mushrooms
- 2 tsp olive oil
- 1 pound ground turkey
- 3 tbsp pesto sauce
- 1 cup diced onion
- 2 cups broccoli florets
- 6 cups zucchini, spiralized

Directions:
1. Heat the oil in a skillet. Add zucchini and cook for 2-3 minutes, stirring continuously; set aside.
2. Add turkey to the skillet and cook until browned, about 7-8 minutes. Transfer to a plate. Add onion and cook until translucent, about 3 minutes. Add broccoli and mushrooms, and cook for 7 more minutes. Return the turkey to the skillet. Stir in the pesto sauce. Cover the pan, lower the heat, and simmer for 15 minutes. Stir in zucchini pasta and serve immediately.

Nutrition Info:
- Per Servings 3.8g Carbs, 19g Protein, 16g Fat, 273 Calories

Basil Turkey Meatballs

Servings: 4
Cooking Time: 15 Minutes

Ingredients:
- 1 pound ground turkey
- 2 tbsp chopped sun-dried tomatoes
- 2 tbsp chopped basil
- ½ tsp garlic powder
- 1 egg
- ½ tsp salt
- ¼ cup almond flour
- 2 tbsp olive oil
- ½ cup shredded mozzarella
- ¼ tsp pepper

Directions:
1. Place everything except the oil in a bowl. Mix with your hands until combined. Form 16 meatballs out of the mixture. Heat the olive oil in a skillet over medium heat. Cook the meatballs for 3 minutes per each side.

Nutrition Info:
- Per Servings 2g Carbs, 22g Protein, 26g Fat, 310 Calories

Chicken Skewers With Celery Fries

Servings: 4
Cooking Time: 60 Minutes

Ingredients:
- 2 chicken breasts
- ½ tsp salt
- ¼ tsp ground black pepper
- 2 tbsp olive oil
- 1/4 chicken broth
- For the fries
- 1 lb celery root
- 2 tbsp olive oil
- ½ tsp salt
- ¼ tsp ground black pepper

Directions:
1. Set an oven to 400ºF. Grease and line a baking sheet. In a large bowl, mix oil, spices and the chicken; set in the fridge for 10 minutes while covered. Peel and chop celery root to form fry shapes and place into a separate bowl. Apply oil to coat and add pepper and salt for seasoning. Arrange to the baking tray in an even layer and bake for 10 minutes.
2. Take the chicken from the refrigerator and thread onto the skewers. Place over the celery, pour in the chicken broth, then set in the oven for 30 minutes. Serve with lemon wedges.

Nutrition Info:
- Per Servings 6g Carbs, 39g Protein, 43g Fat, 579 Calories

Chicken With Green Sauce

Servings: 4
Cooking Time: 35 Minutes

Ingredients:
- 2 tbsp butter
- 4 scallions, chopped
- 4 chicken breasts, skinless and boneless
- Salt and black pepper, to taste
- 6 ounces sour cream
- 2 tbsp fresh dill, chopped

Directions:
1. Heat a pan with the butter over medium-high heat, add in the chicken, season with pepper and salt, and fry for 2-3 per side until golden. Transfer to a baking dish and cook in the oven for 15 minutes at 390ºF, until no longer pink.
2. To the pan add scallions, and cook for 2 minutes. Pour in the sour cream, warm through without boil. Slice the chicken and serve on a platter with green sauce spooned over and fresh dill.

Nutrition Info:
- Per Servings 2.3g Carbs, 18g Protein, 9g Fat, 236 Calories

Stewed Chicken Salsa

Servings: 4
Cooking Time: 25 Minutes

Ingredients:
- 1 cup shredded cheddar cheese
- 8-ounces cream cheese
- 16-ounces salsa
- 4 skinless and boneless thawed chicken breasts
- 4 tablespoons butter
- 1 cup water

Directions:
1. Add all ingredients in a pot, except for sour cream, on high fire, and bring to a boil.
2. Once boiling, lower fire to a simmer and cook for 20 minutes.
3. Adjust seasoning to taste and stir in sour cream.
4. Serve and enjoy.

Nutrition Info:
- Per Servings 9.6g Carbs, 67.8g Protein, 32.6g Fat, 658 Calories

Turkey & Mushroom Bake

Servings: 8
Cooking Time: 55 Minutes

Ingredients:
- 4 cups mushrooms, sliced
- 1 egg, whisked
- 3 cups green cabbage, shredded
- 3 cups turkey meat, cooked and chopped
- ½ cup chicken stock
- ½ cup cream cheese
- 1 tsp poultry seasoning
- 2 cup cheddar cheese, grated
- ½ cup Parmesan cheese, grated
- Salt and ground black pepper, to taste
- ¼ tsp garlic powder

Directions:
1. Set a pan over medium-low heat. Stir in chicken broth, egg, Parmesan cheese, pepper, garlic powder, poultry seasoning, cheddar cheese, cream cheese, and salt, and simmer.
2. Place in the cabbage and turkey meat, and set away from the heat.
3. Add the mushrooms, pepper, turkey mixture and salt in a baking dish and spread. Place aluminum foil to cover, set in an oven at 390°F, and bake for 35 minutes. Allow cooling and enjoy.

Nutrition Info:
- Per Servings 3g Carbs, 25g Protein, 15g Fat, 245 Calories

Grilled Chicken Wings

Servings: 4
Cooking Time: 2 Hours 25 Minutes

Ingredients:
- 2 pounds wings
- Juice from 1 lemon
- ½ cup fresh parsley, chopped
- 2 garlic cloves, peeled and minced
- 1 Serrano pepper, chopped
- 3 tbsp olive oil
- ½ tsp cilantro
- Salt and ground black pepper, to taste
- Lemon wedges, for serving
- Ranch dip, for serving

Directions:
1. Using a bowl, stir together lemon juice, garlic, salt, serrano pepper, cilantro, olive oil, and pepper. Place in the chicken wings and toss well to coat. Refrigerate for 2 hours. Set a grill over high heat and add on the chicken wings; cook each side for 6 minutes. Set the chicken wings on a plate and serve alongside lemon wedges and ranch dip.

Nutrition Info:
- Per Servings 4.3g Carbs, 18.5g Protein, 11.5g Fat, 216 Calories

Chicken Country Style

Servings: 4
Cooking Time: 25 Minutes

Ingredients:
- 3 tablespoons butter
- 1 packet dry Lipton's onion soup mix
- 1 can Campbell's chicken gravy
- 4 skinless and boneless chicken breasts
- 1/3 teaspoon pepper
- 1 cup water

Directions:
1. Add all ingredients in a pot on high fire and bring it to a boil.
2. Once boiling, lower fire to a simmer and cook for 25 minutes.
3. Adjust seasoning to taste.
4. Serve and enjoy.

Nutrition Info:
- Per Servings 6.8g Carbs, 53.7g Protein, 16.9g Fat, 380 Calories

Turkey & Leek Soup

Servings: 4
Cooking Time: 45 Minutes

Ingredients:
- 3 celery stalks, chopped
- 2 leeks, chopped
- 1 tbsp butter
- 6 cups chicken stock
- Salt and ground black pepper, to taste
- ¼ cup fresh parsley, chopped
- 3 cups zoodles
- 3 cups turkey meat, cooked and chopped

Directions:
1. Set a pot over medium-high heat, stir in leeks and celery and cook for 5 minutes. Place in the parsley, turkey meat, pepper, salt, and stock, and cook for 20 minutes. Stir in the zoodles, and cook turkey soup for 5 minutes. Serve in bowls and enjoy.

Nutrition Info:
- Per Servings 3g Carbs, 15g Protein, 11g Fat, 305 Calories

Turkey, Coconut And Kale Chili

Servings: 5
Cooking Time: 30 Minutes

Ingredients:
- 18 ounces turkey breasts, cubed
- 1 cup kale, chopped
- 20 ounces canned diced tomatoes
- 2 tbsp coconut oil
- 2 tbsp coconut cream
- 2 garlic cloves, peeled and minced
- 2 onions, and sliced
- 1 tbsp ground coriander
- 2 tbsp fresh ginger, grated
- 1 tbsp turmeric
- 1 tbsp cumin
- Salt and ground black pepper, to taste
- 2 tbsp chili powder

Directions:

1. Set a pan over medium-high heat and warm the coconut oil, stir in the turkey and onion, and cook for 5 minutes. Place in garlic and ginger, and cook for 1 minute. Stir in the tomatoes, pepper, turmeric, coriander, salt, cumin, and chili powder. Place in the coconut cream, and cook for 10 minutes.

2. Transfer to an immersion blender alongside kale; blend well. Allow simmering, cook for 15 minutes.

Nutrition Info:
- Per Servings 4.2g Carbs, 25g Protein, 15.2g Fat, 295 Calories

One-pot Chicken With Mushrooms And Spinach

Servings: 4
Cooking Time: 40 Minutes

Ingredients:
- 4 chicken thighs
- 2 cups mushrooms, sliced
- 1 cup spinach, chopped
- ¼ cup butter
- Salt and black pepper, to taste
- ½ tsp onion powder
- ½ tsp garlic powder
- ½ cup water
- 1 tsp Dijon mustard
- 1 tbsp fresh tarragon, chopped

Directions:

1. Set a pan over medium-high heat and warm half of the butter, place in the thighs, and sprinkle with onion powder, pepper, garlic powder, and salt. Cook each side for 3 minutes and set on a plate.

2. Place the remaining butter to the same pan and warm. Stir in mushrooms and cook for 5 minutes. Place in water and mustard, take the chicken pieces back to the pan, and cook for 15 minutes while covered. Stir in the tarragon and spinach, and cook for 5 minutes.

Nutrition Info:
- Per Servings 1g Carbs, 32g Protein, 23g Fat, 453 Calories

Chicken Stew With Sun-dried Tomatoes

Servings: 4
Cooking Time: 60 Minutes

Ingredients:
- 2 carrots, chopped
- 2 tbsp olive oil
- 2 celery stalks, chopped
- 2 cups chicken stock
- 1 shallot, chopped
- 28 oz chicken thighs, skinless, boneless
- 3 garlic cloves, peeled and minced
- ½ tsp dried rosemary
- 2 oz sun-dried tomatoes, chopped
- 1 cup spinach
- ¼ tsp dried thyme
- ½ cup heavy cream
- Salt and ground black pepper, to taste
- A pinch of xanthan gum

Directions:

1. In a pot, heat the olive oil over medium heat and add garlic, carrots, celery, and shallot; season with salt and pepper and sauté for 5-6 minutes until tender. Stir in the chicken and cook for 5 minutes.

2. Pour in the stock, tomatoes, rosemary, and thyme, and cook for 30 minutes covered. Stir in xanthan gum, cream, and spinach; cook for 5 minutes. Adjust the seasonings and separate into bowls.

Nutrition Info:
- Per Servings 6g Carbs, 23g Protein, 11g Fat, 224 Calories

Chicken And Spinach Stir Fry

Servings: 4
Cooking Time: 10 Minutes

Ingredients:
- 2 cloves of garlic, minced
- 1 tablespoon fresh ginger, grated
- 1 ¼ pounds boneless chicken breasts, cut into strips
- 2 tablespoons yellow miso, diluted in water
- 2 cups baby spinach
- 2 tablespoons olive oil
- Pepper and salt to taste

Directions:
1. Heat oil in a skillet over medium-high heat and sauté the garlic for 30 seconds until fragrant.
2. Stir in the ginger and chicken breasts. Season lightly with pepper and salt.
3. Cook for 5 minutes while stirring constantly.
4. Stir in the diluted miso paste.
5. Continue cooking for 3 more minutes before adding spinach.
6. Cook for another minute or until the spinach leaves have wilted.

Nutrition Info:
- Per Servings 1.3g Carbs, 32.5g Protein, 10.5g Fat, 237 Calories

Chicken And Spinach

Servings: 8
Cooking Time: 50 Minutes

Ingredients:
- 1-pound chicken breasts
- 2 jars commercial pasta sauce
- 2 cups baby spinach
- 1 onion chopped
- ¼ cup cheese
- 5 tbsps oil
- ½ cup water
- Pepper and salt to taste

Directions:
1. Place a heavy-bottomed pot on medium-high fire and heat pot for 2 minutes.
2. Add oil and swirl to coat sides and bottom of the pot. Heat oil for a minute.
3. Season chicken breasts with pepper and salt. Brown chicken for 4 minutes per side. Transfer to a chopping board and cut into ½-inch cubes.
4. In the same pot, sauté onions for 5 minutes. Add pasta sauce and season with pepper and salt. Stir in water and chicken breasts. Simmer pasta sauce for 30 minutes on low fire. Stir the bottom of the pot every now and then.
5. Mix spinach in a pot of sauce. Let it rest for 5 minutes.

6. Serve and enjoy with a sprinkle of cheese.

Nutrition Info:
- Per Servings 6.7g Carbs, 21.2g Protein, 15.6g Fat, 216 Calories

Sweet Garlic Chicken Skewers

Servings: 4
Cooking Time: 17 Minutes + Time Refrigeration

Ingredients:
- For the Skewers
- 3 tbsp soy sauce
- 1 tbsp ginger-garlic paste
- 2 tbsp swerve brown sugar
- Chili pepper to taste
- 2 tbsp olive oil
- 3 chicken breasts, cut into cubes
- For the Dressing
- ½ cup tahini
- ½ tsp garlic powder
- Pink salt to taste
- ¼ cup warm water

Directions:
1. In a small bowl, whisk the soy sauce, ginger-garlic paste, brown sugar, chili pepper, and olive oil.
2. Put the chicken in a zipper bag, pour the marinade over, seal and shake for an even coat. Marinate in the fridge for 2 hours.
3. Preheat a grill to 400ºF and thread the chicken on skewers. Cook for 10 minutes in total with three to four turnings to be golden brown. Plate them. Mix the tahini, garlic powder, salt, and warm water in a bowl. Pour into serving jars.
4. Serve the chicken skewers and tahini dressing with cauli fried rice.

Nutrition Info:
- Per Servings 2g Carbs, 15g Protein, 17.4g Fat, 225 Calories

Cheesy Chicken Bake With Zucchini

Servings: 12
Cooking Time: 45 Minutes

Ingredients:
- 2 lb chicken breasts, cubed
- 1 tbsp butter
- 1 cup green bell peppers, sliced
- 1 cup yellow onions, sliced
- 1 zucchini, sliced
- 2 garlic cloves, divided
- 2 tsp Italian seasoning
- ½ tsp salt
- ½ tsp black pepper
- 8 oz cream cheese, softened
- ½ cup mayonnaise
- 2 tbsp Worcestershire sauce (sugar-free)
- 2 cups cheddar cheese, shredded

Directions:
1. Set oven to 370ºF and grease and line a baking dish.
2. Set a pan over medium-high heat. Place in the butter and let melt, then add in the chicken.
3. Cook until browned. Place in onions, zucchini, black pepper, garlic, peppers, salt, and 1 tsp of Italian seasonings. Cook until tender. Set aside.
4. In a bowl, mix cream cheese, garlic, cheddar cheese, remaining seasoning, mayonnaise, and Worcestershire sauce. Stir in meat. Place the mixture into the prepared baking dish then set into the oven. Cook until browned for 30 minutes.

Nutrition Info:
- Per Servings 4.5g Carbs, 21g Protein, 37g Fat, 489 Calories

Slow Cooked Chicken Drumstick

Servings: 12
Cooking Time: 7 Hours

Ingredients:
- 12 chicken drumsticks
- 1 ½ tbsp paprika
- ¼ tsp dried thyme
- ½ tsp onion powder
- 2 tbsp Worcestershire sauce
- Salt and pepper to taste
- ½ cup water

Directions:
1. Place all ingredients in the slow cooker. Give a good stir to coat the entire chicken with the spices.
2. Close the slow cooker, press high settings, and cook for 7 hours.
3. Serve and enjoy.

Nutrition Info:
- Per Servings 2.5g Carbs, 23.8g Protein, 12.1g Fat, 218 Calories

Grilled Paprika Chicken With Steamed Broccoli

Servings: 6
Cooking Time: 17 Minutes

Ingredients:
- Cooking spray
- 3 tbsp smoked paprika
- Salt and black pepper to taste
- 2 tsp garlic powder
- 1 tbsp olive oil
- 6 chicken breasts
- 1 head broccoli, cut into florets

Directions:
1. Place broccoli florets onto the steamer basket over the boiling water; steam approximately 8 minutes or until crisp-tender. Set aside. Grease grill grate with cooking spray and preheat to 400ºF.
2. Combine paprika, salt, black pepper, and garlic powder in a bowl. Brush chicken with olive oil and sprinkle spice mixture over and massage with hands.
3. Grill chicken for 7 minutes per side until well-cooked, and plate. Serve warm with steamed broccoli.

Nutrition Info:
- Per Servings 2g Carbs, 26g Protein, 35.3g Fat, 422 Calories

Sticky Cranberry Chicken Wings

Servings: 6
Cooking Time: 50 Minutes

Ingredients:
- 2 lb chicken wings
- 4 tbsp unsweetened cranberry puree
- 2 tbsp olive oil
- Salt to taste
- Sweet chili sauce to taste
- Lemon juice from 1 lemon

Directions:
1. Preheat the oven (broiler side) to 400ºF. Then, in a bowl, mix the cranberry puree, olive oil, salt, sweet chili sauce, and lemon juice. After, add in the wings and toss to coat.
2. Place the chicken under the broiler, and cook for 45 minutes, turning once halfway.
3. Remove the chicken after and serve warm with a cranberry and cheese dipping sauce.

Nutrition Info:
- Per Servings 1.6g Carbs, 17.6g Protein, 8.5g Fat, 152 Calories

Easy Chicken Vindaloo

Servings: 5
Cooking Time: 30 Minutes

Ingredients:

- 1 lb. chicken thighs, skin and bones not removed
- 2 tbsp. garam masala
- 6 whole red dried chilies
- 1 onion, sliced
- 5 cloves of garlic, crushed
- Pepper and salt to taste
- 1 tsp oil
- 1 cup water

Directions:

1. On high fire, heat a saucepan for 2 minutes. Add oil to the pan and swirl to coat bottom and sides. Heat oil for a minute.
2. Add chicken with skin side touching pan and sear for 5 minutes. Turn chicken over and sear the other side for 3 minutes. Transfer chicken to a plate.
3. In the same pan, sauté garlic for a minute. Add onion and sauté for 3 minutes. Stir in garam masala and chilies.
4. Return chicken to the pot and mix well. Add water and season with pepper and salt.
5. Cover and lower fire to simmer and cook for 15 minutes.
6. Serve and enjoy.

Nutrition Info:

- Per Servings 1.4g Carbs, 15.2g Protein, 15.1g Fat, 206 Calories

Turkey Enchilada Bowl

Servings: 4
Cooking Time: 30 Minutes

Ingredients:

- 2 tbsp coconut oil
- 1 lb boneless, skinless turkey thighs, cut into pieces
- ¾ cup red enchilada sauce (sugar-free)
- ¼ cup water
- ¼ cup chopped onion
- 3 oz canned diced green chilis
- 1 avocado, diced
- 1 cup shredded mozzarella cheese
- ¼ cup chopped pickled jalapeños
- ½ cup sour cream
- 1 tomato, diced

Directions:

1. Set a large pan over medium-high heat. Add coconut oil and warm. Place in the turkey and cook until browned on the outside. Stir in onion, chillis, water, and enchilada sauce, then close with a lid.
2. Allow simmering for 20 minutes until the turkey is cooked through. Spoon the turkey on a serving bowl and top with the sauce, cheese, sour cream, tomato, and avocado.

Nutrition Info:

- Per Servings 5.9g Carbs, 38g Protein, 40.2g Fat, 568 Calories

Chicken With Monterey Jack Cheese

Servings: 3
Cooking Time: 30 Minutes

Ingredients:

- 2 tbsp butter
- 1 tsp garlic, minced
- 1 pound chicken breasts
- 1 tsp creole seasoning
- ¼ cup scallions, chopped
- ½ cup tomatoes, chopped
- ½ cup chicken stock
- ¼ cup whipping cream
- ½ cup Monterey Jack cheese, grated
- ¼ cup fresh cilantro, chopped
- Salt and black pepper, to taste
- 4 ounces cream cheese
- 8 eggs
- A pinch of garlic powder

Directions:

1. Set a pan over medium heat and warm 1 tbsp butter. Add chicken, season with creole seasoning and cook each side for 2 minutes; remove to a plate. Melt the rest of the butter and stir in garlic and tomatoes; cook for 4 minutes. Return the chicken to the pan and pour in stock; cook for 15 minutes. Place in whipping cream, scallions, salt, Monterey Jack cheese, and pepper; cook for 2 minutes.
2. In a blender, combine the cream cheese with garlic powder, salt, eggs, and pepper, and pulse well. Place the mixture into a lined baking sheet, and then bake for 10 minutes in the oven at 325ºF. Allow the cheese sheet to cool down, place on a cutting board, roll, and slice into medium slices. Split the slices among bowls and top with chicken mixture. Sprinkle with chopped cilantro to serve.

Nutrition Info:

- Per Servings 4g Carbs, 39g Protein, 34g Fat, 445 Calories

Turkey & Cheese Stuffed Mushrooms

Servings: 5
Cooking Time: 20 Minutes

Ingredients:
- 12 ounces button mushroom caps
- 3 ounces cream cheese
- ¼ cup carrot, chopped
- 1 tsp ranch seasoning mix
- 4 tbsp hot sauce
- ¾ cup blue cheese, crumbled
- ¼ cup onion, chopped
- ½ cup turkey breasts, cooked, chopped
- Salt and black pepper, to taste
- Cooking spray

Directions:
1. Using a bowl, combine the cream cheese with the blue cheese, ranch seasoning, turkey, onion, carrot, salt, hot sauce, and pepper. Stuff each mushroom cap with this mixture, set on a lined baking sheet, spray with cooking spray, place in the oven at 425ºF, and bake for 10 minutes.

Nutrition Info:
- Per Servings 8.6g Carbs, 51g Protein, 17g Fat, 486 Calories

Stuffed Avocados With Chicken

Servings: 2
Cooking Time: 10 Minutes

Ingredients:
- 2 avocados, cut in half and pitted
- ¼ cup pesto
- 1 tsp dried thyme
- 2 tbsp cream cheese
- 1½ cups chicken, cooked and shredded
- Salt and ground black pepper, to taste
- ¼ tsp cayenne pepper
- ½ tsp onion powder
- ½ tsp garlic powder
- 1 tsp paprika
- Salt and black pepper, to taste
- 2 tbsp lemon juice

Directions:
1. Scoop the insides of the avocado halves, and place the flesh in a bowl. Add in the chicken. Stir in the remaining ingredients. Stuff the avocado cups with chicken mixture and enjoy.

Nutrition Info:
- Per Servings 5g Carbs, 24g Protein, 40g Fat, 511 Calories

Homemade Chicken Pizza Calzone

Servings: 4
Cooking Time: 60 Minutes

Ingredients:
- 2 eggs
- 1 low carb pizza crust
- ½ cup Pecorino cheese, grated
- 1 lb chicken breasts, skinless, boneless, halved
- ½ cup sugar-free marinara sauce
- 1 tsp Italian seasoning
- 1 tsp onion powder
- 1 tsp garlic powder
- Salt and black pepper, to taste
- ¼ cup flax seed, ground
- 6 ounces provolone cheese

Directions:
1. Using a bowl, combine the Italian seasoning with onion powder, salt, Pecorino cheese, pepper, garlic powder, and flax seed. In a separate bowl, combine the eggs with pepper and salt.
2. Dip the chicken pieces in eggs, and then in seasoning mixture, lay all parts on a lined baking sheet, and bake for 25 minutes in the oven at 390º F.
3. Place the pizza crust dough on a lined baking sheet and spread half of the provolone cheese on half. Remove chicken from oven, chop it, and scatter it over the provolone cheese. Spread over the marinara sauce and top with the remaining cheese.
4. Cover with the other half of the dough and shape the pizza in a calzone. Seal the edges, set in the oven and bake for 20 minutes. Allow the calzone to cool down before slicing and enjoy.

Nutrition Info:
- Per Servings 4.6g Carbs, 28g Protein, 15g Fat, 425 Calories

Fish And Seafood Recipes

Fish And Seafood Recipes

Asian Seafood Stir-fry

Serves: 4
Cooking Time: 15 Minutes

Ingredients:
- 4 teaspoons sesame oil
- 1/2 cup yellow onion, sliced
- 1 cup asparagus spears, sliced
- 1/2 cup celery, chopped
- 1/2 cup enoki mushrooms
- 1 pound bay scallops
- 1 tablespoon fresh parsley, chopped
- Kosher salt and ground black pepper, to taste
- 1/2 teaspoon red pepper flakes, crushed
- 1 tablespoon coconut aminos
- 2 tablespoons rice wine
- 1/2 cup dry roasted peanuts, roughly chopped

Directions:
1. Heat 1 teaspoon of the sesame oil in a wok over a medium-high flame. Now, fry the onion until crisp-tender and translucent; reserve.
2. Heat another teaspoon of the sesame oil and fry the asparagus and celery for about 3 minutes until crisp-tender; reserve.
3. Then, heat another teaspoon of the sesame oil and cook the mushrooms for 2 minutes more or until they start to soften; reserve.
4. Lastly, heat the remaining teaspoon of sesame oil and cook the bay scallops just until they are opaque.
5. Return all reserved vegetables to the wok. Add in the remaining ingredients and toss to combine. Serve warm and enjoy!

Nutrition Info:
- Per Serves 5.9g Carbs; 27g Protein; 12.5g Fat; 236 Calories

Steamed Asparagus And Shrimps

Servings: 6
Cooking Time: 15 Minutes

Ingredients:
- 1-pound shrimps, peeled and deveined
- 1 bunch asparagus, trimmed
- ½ tablespoon Cajun seasoning
- 2 tablespoons butter
- 5 tablespoons oil
- Salt and pepper to taste

Directions:
1. In a heat-proof dish that fits inside the saucepan, add all ingredients. Mix well.
2. Place a large saucepan on the medium-high fire. Place a trivet inside the saucepan and fill the pan halfway with water. Cover and bring to a boil.
3. Cover dish with foil and place on a trivet.
4. Cover pan and steam for 10 minutes. Let it rest in pan for another 5 minutes.
5. Serve and enjoy.

Nutrition Info:
- Per Servings 1.1g Carbs, 15.5g Protein, 15.8g Fat, 204.8 Calories

Chili-garlic Salmon

Servings: 4
Cooking Time: 15 Minutes

Ingredients:
- 5 tbsp. sweet chili sauce
- ¼ cup coconut aminos
- 4 salmon fillets
- 3 tbsp. green onions, chopped
- 3 cloves garlic, peeled and minced
- Pepper to taste

Directions:
1. Place a trivet in a large saucepan and pour a cup or two of water into the pan. Bring to a boil.
2. In a small bowl, whisk well sweet chili sauce, garlic, and coconut aminos.
3. Place salmon in a heatproof dish that fits inside a saucepan. Season salmon with pepper. Drizzle with sweet chili sauce mixture. Sprinkle green onions on top of the filet.
4. Seal dish with foil. Place the dish on the trivet inside the saucepan. Cover and steam for 15 minutes.
5. Serve and enjoy.

Nutrition Info:
- Per Servings 0.9g Carbs, 65.4g Protein, 14.4g Fat, 409 Calories

Air Fryer Seasoned Salmon Fillets

Servings: 4
Cooking Time: 10 Mins

Ingredients:

- 2 lbs. salmon fillets
- 1 tsp. stevia
- 2 tbsp. whole grain mustard
- 1 clove of garlic, minced
- 1/2 tsp. thyme leaves
- 2 tsp. extra-virgin olive oil
- Cooking spray
- Salt and black pepper to taste

Directions:

1. Preheat your Air Fryer to 390 degrees F.
2. Season salmon fillets with salt and pepper.
3. Add together the mustard, garlic, stevia, thyme, and oil in a bowl, stir to combined well. Rub the seasoning mixture on top of salmon fillets.
4. Spray the Air Fryer basket with cooking spray and cook seasoned fillets for 10 minutes until crispy. Let it cool before serving.

Nutrition Info:

- Per Servings 14g Carbs, 18g Protein, 10g Fat, 238 Calories

Asian-style Fish Salad

Serves: 2
Cooking Time: 15 Minutes

Ingredients:

- Salad:
- 1/4 cup water
- 1/4 cup Sauvignon Blanc
- 1/2 pound salmon fillets
- 1 cup Chinese cabbage, sliced
- 1 tomato, sliced
- 2 radishes, sliced
- 1 bell pepper, sliced
- 1 medium-sized white onion, sliced
- Salad Dressing:
- 1/2 teaspoon fresh garlic, minced
- 1 fresh chili pepper, seeded and minced
- 1/2 teaspoon fresh ginger, peeled and grated
- 2 tablespoons fresh lime juice
- 1 tablespoon sesame oil
- 1 tablespoon tamari sauce
- 1 teaspoon xylitol
- 1 tablespoon fresh mint, roughly chopped
- Sea salt and freshly ground black pepper, to taste

Directions:

1. Place the water and Sauvignon Blanc in a sauté pan; bring to a simmer over moderate heat.

2. Place the salmon fillets, skin-side down in the pan and cover with the lid. Cook for 5 to 8 minutes or to your desired doneness; do not overcook the salmon; reserve.
3. Place the Chinese cabbage, tomato, radishes, bell pepper, and onion in a serving bowl.
4. Prepare the salad dressing by whisking all ingredients. Dress your salad, top with the salmon fillets and serve immediately!

Nutrition Info:

- Per Serves4.9g Carbs; 24.4g Protein; 15.1g Fat; 277 Calories

Baked Codfish With Lemon

Serves: 4
Cooking Time:25 Minutes

Ingredients:

- 4 fillets codfish
- 1 teaspoon salt
- 1 teaspoon pepper
- 2 tablespoons olive oil
- 2 teaspoons dried basil
- 2 tablespoons melted butter
- 1 teaspoon dried thyme
- 1/3 teaspoon onion powder
- 2 lemons, juiced
- lemon wedges, for garnish

Directions:

1. Preheat the oven to 400°F.
2. In a medium bowl combine the lemon juice, onion powder, olive oil, dried basil and thyme. Stir well. Season the fillets with salt and pepper.
3. Top each fillet into the mixture. Then place the fillets into a medium baking dish, greased with melted butter.
4. Bake the codfish fillets for 15-20 minutes. Serve with fresh lemon wedges. Enjoy!

Nutrition Info:

- Per serving: 3.9g Carbs; 21.2g Protein; 23.6g Fat; 308 Calories

Asian-style Steamed Mussels

Serves:6
Cooking Time:25 Minutes

Ingredients:

- 5 tbsp sesame oil
- 1 onion, chopped
- 3 lb mussels, cleaned
- 2 garlic cloves, minced
- 12 oz coconut milk
- 16 oz white wine
- 1 lime, juiced
- 2 tsp red curry powder

- 2 tbsp cilantro, chopped

Directions:

1. Warm the sesame oil in a saucepan over medium heat and cook onion and garlic cloves for 3 minutes. Pour in wine, coconut milk, and curry powder and cook for 5 minutes. Add mussels, turn off the heat, cover the saucepan, and steam the mussels until the shells open up, 5 minutes. Discard any closed mussels. Top with cilantro and serve.

Nutrition Info:

- Per Serves 5.4g Carbs ; 28.2g Protein:16g Fat ; 323 Calories

Chili-lime Shrimps

Servings: 4
Cooking Time: 10 Minutes

Ingredients:

- 1 ½ lb. raw shrimp, peeled and deveined
- 1 tbsp. chili flakes
- 5 tbsp sweet chili sauce
- 2 tbsp. lime juice, freshly squeezed
- 1 tsp cayenne pepper
- Salt and pepper to taste
- 5 tbsp oil
- 3 tbsp water

Directions:

1. In a small bowl, whisk well chili flakes, sweet chili sauce, cayenne pepper, and water.
2. On medium-high fire, heat a nonstick saucepan for 2 minutes. Add oil to a pan and swirl to coat bottom and sides. Heat oil for a minute.
3. Stir fry shrimp, around 5 minutes. Season lightly with salt and pepper.
4. Stir in sweet chili mixture and toss well shrimp to coat.
5. Turn off fire, drizzle lime juice and toss well to coat.
6. Serve and enjoy.

Nutrition Info:

- Per Servings 1.7g Carbs, 34.9g Protein, 19.8g Fat, 306 Calories

Simple Steamed Salmon Fillets

Servings: 3
Cooking Time: 15 Minutes

Ingredients:

- 10 oz. salmon fillets
- 2 tbsp. coconut aminos
- 2 tbsp. lemon juice, freshly squeezed
- 1 tsp. sesame seeds, toasted
- 3 tbsp sesame oil
- Salt and pepper to taste

Directions:

1. Place a trivet in a large saucepan and pour a cup or two of water into the pan. Bring to a boil.
2. Place salmon in a heatproof dish that fits inside the saucepan. Season salmon with pepper and salt. Drizzle with coconut aminos, lemon juice, sesame oil, and sesame seeds.
3. Seal dish with foil. Place the dish on the trivet inside the saucepan. Cover and steam for 15 minutes.
4. Serve and enjoy.

Nutrition Info:

- Per Servings 2.6g Carbs, 20.1g Protein, 17.4g Fat, 210 Calories

Steamed Cod With Ginger

Servings: 4
Cooking Time: 15 Minutes

Ingredients:

- 4 cod fillets, skin removed
- 3 tbsp. lemon juice, freshly squeezed
- 2 tbsp. coconut aminos
- 2 tbsp. grated ginger
- 6 scallions, chopped
- 5 tbsp coconut oil
- Pepper and salt to taste

Directions:

1. Place a trivet in a large saucepan and pour a cup or two of water into the pan. Bring to a boil.
2. In a small bowl, whisk well lemon juice, coconut aminos, coconut oil, and grated ginger.
3. Place scallions in a heatproof dish that fits inside a saucepan. Season scallions mon with pepper and salt. Drizzle with ginger mixture. Sprinkle scallions on top.
4. Seal dish with foil. Place the dish on the trivet inside the saucepan. Cover and steam for 15 minutes.
5. Serve and enjoy.

Nutrition Info:

- Per Servings 10g Carbs, 28.3g Protein, 40g Fat, 514 Calories

Avocado Salad With Shrimp

Serves: 4
Cooking Time:10 Minutes

Ingredients:

- 2 tomatoes, sliced into cubes
- 2 medium avocados, cut into large pieces
- 3 tablespoons red onion, diced
- ½ large lettuce, chopped
- 2 lbs. shrimp, peeled and deveined
- For the Lime Vinaigrette Dressing
- 2 cloves garlic, minced
- 1 ½ teaspoon Dijon mustard
- 1/3 cup extra virgin olive oil
- salt and pepper to taste

- 1/3 cup lime juice

Directions:

1. Add the peeled and deveined shrimp and 2 quarts of water to a cooking pot and print to a boil, lower the heat and let them simmer for 1-2 minutes until the shrimp is pink. Set aside and let them cool.

2. Next add the chopped lettuce in a large bowl. Then add the avocado, tomatoes, shrimp and red onion.

3. In a small bowl whisk together the Dijon mustard, garlic, olive oil and lime juice. Mix well.

4. Pour the lime vinaigrette dressing over the salad and serve.

Nutrition Info:

- Per serving: 7g Carbs; 43.5g Protein; 17.6g Fat; 377 Calories;

Sicilian-style Zoodle Spaghetti

Servings: 2
Cooking Time: 10 Minutes

Ingredients:

- 4 cups zoodles (spiralled zucchini)
- 2 ounces cubed bacon
- 4 ounces canned sardines, chopped
- ½ cup canned chopped tomatoes
- 1 tbsp capers
- 1 tbsp parsley
- 1 tsp minced garlic

Directions:

1. Pour some of the sardine oil in a pan. Add garlic and cook for 1 minute. Add the bacon and cook for 2 more minutes. Stir in the tomatoes and let simmer for 5 minutes. Add zoodles and sardines and cook for 3 minutes.

Nutrition Info:

- Per Servings 6g Carbs, 20g Protein, 31g Fat, 355 Calories

Five-spice Steamed Tilapia

Servings: 4
Cooking Time: 15 Minutes

Ingredients:

- 1 lb. Tilapia fillets,
- 1 tsp. Chinese five-spice powder
- 3 tablespoons coconut oil
- 3 scallions, sliced thinly
- Salt and pepper to taste

Directions:

1. Place a trivet in a large saucepan and pour a cup of water into the pan. Bring to a boil.

2. Place tilapia in a heatproof dish that fits inside a saucepan. Drizzle oil on tilapia. Season with salt, pepper, and Chinese five-spice powder. Garnish with scallions.

3. Seal dish with foil. Place the dish on the trivet inside the saucepan. Cover and steam for 15 minutes.

4. Serve and enjoy.

Nutrition Info:

- Per Servings 0.9g Carbs, 24g Protein, 12.3g Fat, 201 Calories

Bacon Wrapped Mahi-mahi

Serves: 2
Cooking Time: 12 Minutes

Ingredients:

- 2 fillets of mahi-mahi
- 2 strips of bacon
- ½ of lime, zested
- 4 basil leaves
- ½ tsp salt
- Seasoning:
- ½ tsp ground black pepper
- 1 tbsp avocado oil

Directions:

1. Turn on the oven, then set it to 375 °F and let them preheat.Meanwhile, season fillets with salt and black pepper, top each fillet with 2 basil leaves, sprinkle with lime zest, wrap with a bacon strip and secure with a toothpick if needed.Take a medium skillet pan, place it over medium-high heat, add oil and when hot, place prepared fillets in it and cook for 2 minutes per side.Transfer pan into the oven and bake the fish for 5 to 7 minutes until thoroughly cooked. Serve.

Nutrition Info:

- 1.2 g Carbs; 27.1 g Protein; 11.3 g Fats; 217 Calories

Baked Calamari And Shrimp

Serves: 1
Cooking Time: 20 Minutes

Ingredients:

- 8 ounces calamari, cut in medium rings
- 7 ounces shrimp, peeled and deveined
- 1 eggs
- 3 tablespoons coconut flour
- 1 tablespoon coconut oil
- 2 tablespoons avocado, chopped
- 1 teaspoon tomato paste
- 1 tablespoon mayonnaise
- A splash of Worcestershire sauce
- 1 teaspoon lemon juice
- 2 lemon slices
- Salt and black pepper to the taste
- ½ teaspoon turmeric

Directions:

1. In a bowl, whisk egg with coconut oil.

2. Add calamari rings and shrimp and toss to coat.

3. In another bowl, mix flour with salt, pepper and turmeric and stir.

4. Dredge calamari and shrimp in this mix, place everything on a lined baking sheet, introduce in the oven at 400 °F and bake for 10 minutes.

5. Flip calamari and shrimp and bake for 10 minutes more.

6. Meanwhile, in a bowl, mix avocado with mayo and tomato paste and mash using a fork.

7. Add Worcestershire sauce, lemon juice, salt and pepper and stir well.

8. Divide baked calamari and shrimp on plates and serve with the sauce and lemon juice on the side.

9. Enjoy!

Nutrition Info:
• 10 carbs; 34 protein; 23 fat; 368 calories

Sour Cream Salmon With Parmesan

Servings: 4
Cooking Time: 25 Minutes

Ingredients:
• 1 cup sour cream
• ½ tbsp minced dill
• ½ lemon, zested and juiced
• Pink salt and black pepper to season
• 4 salmon steaks
• ½ cup grated Parmesan cheese

Directions:
1. Preheat oven to 400°F and line a baking sheet with parchment paper; set aside. In a bowl, mix the sour cream, dill, lemon zest, juice, salt and pepper, and set aside.

2. Season the fish with salt and black pepper, drizzle lemon juice on both sides of the fish and arrange them in the baking sheet. Spread the sour cream mixture on each fish and sprinkle with Parmesan.

3. Bake the fish for 15 minutes and after broil the top for 2 minutes with a close watch for a nice a brown color. Plate the fish and serve with buttery green beans.

Nutrition Info:
• Per Servings 1.2g Carbs, 16.2g Protein, 23.4g Fat, 288 Calories

Enchilada Sauce On Mahi Mahi

Servings: 2
Cooking Time: 15 Minutes

Ingredients:
• 2 Mahi fillets, fresh
• ¼ cup commercial enchilada sauce
• Pepper to taste

Directions:
1. In a heat-proof dish that fits inside saucepan, place fish and top with enchilada sauce.

2. Place a large saucepan on the medium-high fire. Place a trivet inside the saucepan and fill the pan halfway with water. Cover and bring to a boil.

3. Cover dish with foil and place on a trivet.

4. Cover pan and steam for 10 minutes. Let it rest in pan for another 5 minutes.

5. Serve and enjoy topped with pepper.

Nutrition Info:
• Per Servings 8.9g Carbs, 19.8g Protein, 15.9g Fat, 257 Calories

Bang Bang Shrimps

Serves: 2
Cooking Time: 6 Minutes

Ingredients:
• 4 oz shrimps¼ tsp paprika
• ¼ tsp apple cider vinegar
• 2 tbsp sweet chili sauce
• ¼ cup mayonnaise
• Seasoning:
• ¼ tsp salt
• 1/8 tsp ground black pepper
• 2 tsp avocado oil

Directions:
1. Take a medium skillet pan, place it over medium heat, add oil and wait until it gets hot.Season shrimps with salt, black pepper, and paprika until coated, add them to the pan, and cook for 2 to 3 minutes per side until pink and cooked.Take a medium bowl, place mayonnaise in it, and then whisk in vinegar and chili sauce until combined.Add shrimps into the mayonnaise mixture, toss until coated, and then serve.

Nutrition Info:
• 7.2 g Carbs; 13 g Protein; 23.1 g Fats; 290 Calories

Parmesan Fish Bake

Servings: 4
Cooking Time: 40 Minutes

Ingredients:
• Cooking spray
• 2 salmon fillets, cubed
• 3 white fish, cubed
• 1 broccoli, cut into florets
• 1 tbsp butter, melted
• Pink salt and black pepper to taste
• 1 cup crème fraiche
• ¼ cup grated Parmesan cheese
• Grated Parmesan cheese for topping

Directions:
1. Preheat oven to 400°F and grease an 8 x 8 inches cas-

serole dish with cooking spray. Toss the fish cubes and broccoli in butter and season with salt and pepper to taste. Spread in the greased dish.

2. Mix the crème fraiche with Parmesan cheese, pour and smear the cream on the fish, and sprinkle with some more Parmesan. Bake for 25 to 30 minutes until golden brown on top, take the dish out, sit for 5 minutes and spoon into plates. Serve with lemon-mustard asparagus.

Nutrition Info:
• Per Servings 4g Carbs, 28g Protein, 17g Fat, 354 Calories

Halibut With Pesto

Servings: 4
Cooking Time: 15 Minutes

Ingredients:
• 4 halibut fillets
• 1 cup basil leaves
• 2 cloves of garlic, minced
• 1 tbsp. lemon juice, freshly squeezed
• 2 tbsp pine nuts
• 2 tbsp. oil, preferably extra virgin olive oil
• Salt and pepper to taste

Directions:
1. In a food processor, pulse the basil, olive oil, pine nuts, garlic, and lemon juice until coarse. Season with salt and pepper to taste.
2. Place a trivet in a large saucepan and pour a cup or two of water into the pan. Bring to a boil.
3. Place salmon in a heatproof dish that fits inside a saucepan. Season salmon with pepper and salt. Drizzle with pesto sauce.
4. Seal dish with foil. Place the dish on the trivet inside the saucepan. Cover and steam for 15 minutes.
5. Serve and enjoy.

Nutrition Info:
• Per Servings 0.8g Carbs, 75.8g Protein, 8.4g Fat, 401 Calories

Cod With Balsamic Tomatoes

Servings: 4
Cooking Time: 30 Minutes

Ingredients:
• 4 center-cut bacon strips, chopped
• 4 cod fillets
• 2 cups grape tomatoes, halved
• 2 tablespoons balsamic vinegar
• 4 tablespoons olive oil
• 1/2 teaspoon salt
• 1/4 teaspoon pepper

Directions:

1. In a large skillet, heat olive oil and cook bacon over medium heat until crisp, stirring occasionally.
2. Remove with a slotted spoon; drain on paper towels.
3. Sprinkle fillets with salt and pepper. Add fillets to bacon drippings; cook over medium-high heat until fish just begins to flake easily with a fork, 4-6 minutes on each side. Remove and keep warm.
4. Add tomatoes to skillet; cook and stir until tomatoes are softened, 2-4 minutes. Stir in vinegar; reduce heat to medium-low. Cook until sauce is thickened, 1-2 minutes longer.
5. Serve cod with tomato mixture and bacon.

Nutrition Info:
• Per Servings 5g Carbs, 26g Protein, 30.4g Fat, 442 Calories

Cilantro Shrimp

Servings: 4
Cooking Time: 10 Minutes

Ingredients:
• 1/2 cup reduced-fat Asian sesame salad dressing
• 1-pound uncooked shrimp, peeled and deveined
• Lime wedges
• 1/4 cup chopped fresh cilantro
• 5 tablespoon olive oil
• Salt and pepper

Directions:
1. In a large nonstick skillet, heat 1 tablespoon dressing over medium heat. Add shrimp; cook and stir 1 minute.
2. Stir in remaining dressing; cook, uncovered, until shrimp turn pink, 1-2 minutes longer.
3. To serve, squeeze lime juice over the top; sprinkle with cilantro, pepper, and salt. If desired, serve with rice.

Nutrition Info:
• Per Servings 4.7g Carbs, 32g Protein, 39g Fat, 509 Calories

Rosemary-lemon Shrimps

Servings: 4
Cooking Time: 8 Minutes

Ingredients:
• 5 tablespoons butter
• ½ cup lemon juice, freshly squeezed
• 1 ½ lb. shrimps, peeled and deveined
• ¼ cup coconut aminos
• 1 tsp rosemary
• Pepper to taste

Directions:
1. Place all ingredients in a large pan on a high fire.
2. Boil for 8 minutes or until shrimps are pink.
3. Serve and enjoy.

Nutrition Info:

- Per Servings 3.7g Carbs, 35.8g Protein, 17.9g Fat, 315 Calories

Coconut Milk Sauce Over Crabs

Servings: 6
Cooking Time: 20 Minutes

Ingredients:
- 2-pounds crab quartered
- 1 can coconut milk
- 1 thumb-size ginger, sliced
- 1 onion, chopped
- 3 cloves of garlic, minced
- Pepper and salt to taste

Directions:
1. Place a heavy-bottomed pot on medium-high fire and add all ingredients.
2. Cover and bring to a boil, lower fire to a simmer, and simmer for 20 minutes.
3. Serve and enjoy.

Nutrition Info:
- Per Servings 6.3g Carbs, 29.3g Protein, 11.3g Fat, 244.1 Calories

Seasoned Salmon With Parmesan

Servings: 4
Cooking Time: 20 Mins

Ingredients:
- 2 lbs. salmon fillet
- 3 minced garlic cloves
- ¼ cup. chopped parsley
- ½ cup. grated parmesan cheese
- Salt and pepper to taste

Directions:
1. Preheat oven to 425 degrees F. Line a baking sheet with parchment paper.
2. Lay salmon fillets on the lined baking sheet, season with salt and pepper to taste.
3. Bake for 10 minutes. Remove from the oven and sprinkle with garlic, parmesan and parsley.
4. Place in the oven to cook for 5 more minutes. Transfer to plates before serving.

Nutrition Info:
- Per Servings 0.6g Carbs, 25g Protein, 12g Fat, 210 Calories

Sautéed Savory Shrimps

Servings: 8
Cooking Time: 15 Minutes

Ingredients:
- 2 pounds shrimp, peeled and deveined

- 4 cloves garlic, minced
- ½ cup chicken stock, low sodium
- 1 tablespoon lemon juice
- Salt and pepper
- 5 tablespoons oil

Directions:
1. Place a heavy-bottomed pot on medium-high fire and heat pot for 3 minutes.
2. Once hot, add oil and stir around to coat pot with oil.
3. Sauté the garlic and corn for 5 minutes.
4. Add remaining ingredients and mix well.
5. Cover and bring to a boil, lower fire to a simmer, and simmer for 5 minutes.
6. Serve and enjoy.

Nutrition Info:
- Per Servings 1.7g Carbs, 25.2g Protein, 9.8g Fat, 182.6 Calories

Baked Fish With Feta And Tomato

Serves: 2
Cooking Time: 15 Minutes

Ingredients:
- 2 pacific whitening fillets
- 1 scallion, chopped
- 1 Roma tomato, chopped
- 1 tsp fresh oregano
- 1-ounce feta cheese, crumbled
- Seasoning:
- 2 tbsp avocado oil
- 1/3 tsp salt
- 1/4 tsp ground black pepper
- ¼ crushed red pepper

Directions:
1. Turn on the oven, then set it to 400 °F and let it preheat. Take a medium skillet pan, place it over medium heat, add oil and when hot, add scallion and cook for 3 minutes. Add tomatoes, stir in ½ tsp oregano, 1/8 tsp salt, black pepper, red pepper, pour in ¼ cup water and bring it to simmer. Sprinkle remaining salt over fillets, add to the pan, drizzle with remaining oil, and then bake for 10 to 12 minutes until fillets are fork-tender. When done, top fish with remaining oregano and cheese and then serve.

Nutrition Info:
- 8 g Carbs; 26.7 g Protein; 29.5 g Fats; 427.5 Calories

Lemon Marinated Salmon With Spices

Servings: 2
Cooking Time: 15 Minutes

Ingredients:

- 2 tablespoons. lemon juice
- 1 tablespoon. yellow miso paste
- 2 teaspoons. Dijon mustard
- 1 pinch cayenne pepper and sea salt to taste
- 2 center-cut salmon fillets, boned; skin on
- 1 1/2 tablespoons mayonnaise
- 1 tablespoon ground black pepper

Directions:

1. In a bowl, combine lemon juice with black pepper. Stir in mayonnaise, miso paste, Dijon mustard, and cayenne pepper, mix well. Pour over salmon fillets, reserve about a tablespoon marinade. Cover and marinate the fish in the refrigerator for 30 minutes.
2. Preheat oven to 450 degrees F. Line a baking sheet with parchment paper.
3. Lay fillets on the prepared baking sheet. Rub the reserved lemon-pepper marinade on fillets. Then season with cayenne pepper and sea salt to taste.
4. Bake in the oven for 10 to 15 minutes until cooked through.

Nutrition Info:

- Per Servings 7.1g Carbs, 20g Protein, 28.1g Fat, 361 Calories

Avocado Tuna Boats

Serves: 2
Cooking Time: 10 Minutes

Ingredients:

- 4 oz tuna, packed in water, drained1 green onion sliced
- 1 avocado, halved, pitted
- 3 tbsp mayonnaise
- 1/3 tsp salt
- Seasoning:
- ¼ tsp ground black pepper
- ¼ tsp paprika

Directions:

1. Prepare the filling and for this, take a medium bowl, place tuna in it, add green onion, salt, black pepper, paprika and mayonnaise and then stir until well combined.Cut avocado in half lengthwise, then remove the pit and fill with prepared filling.Serve.

Nutrition Info:

- ; 7 g Carbs; 8 g Protein; 19 g Fats; 244 Calories

Seared Scallops With Chorizo And Asiago Cheese

Servings: 4
Cooking Time: 15 Minutes

Ingredients:

- 2 tbsp ghee
- 16 fresh scallops
- 8 ounces chorizo, chopped
- 1 red bell pepper, seeds removed, sliced
- 1 cup red onions, finely chopped
- 1 cup asiago cheese, grated
- Salt and black pepper to taste

Directions:

1. Melt half of the ghee in a skillet over medium heat, and cook the onion and bell pepper for 5 minutes until tender. Add the chorizo and stir-fry for another 3 minutes. Remove and set aside.
2. Pat dry the scallops with paper towels, and season with salt and pepper. Add the remaining ghee to the skillet and sear the scallops for 2 minutes on each side to have a golden brown color. Add the chorizo mixture back and warm through. Transfer to serving platter and top with asiago cheese.

Nutrition Info:

- Per Servings 5g Carbs, 36g Protein, 32g Fat, 491 Calories

Avocado & Cauliflower Salad With Prawns

Serves 6
Cooking Time 30 Minutes

Ingredients:

- 1 cauliflower head, florets only
- 1 lb medium-sized prawns
- ¼ cup + 1 tbsp olive oil
- 1 avocado, chopped
- 3 tbsp chopped dill
- ¼ cup lemon juice
- 2 tbsp lemon zest

Directions:

1. Heat 1 tbsp olive oil in a skillet and cook the prawns for 8-10 minutes. Microwave cauliflower for 5 minutes. Place prawns, cauliflower, and avocado in a large bowl. Whisk together the remaining olive oil, lemon zest, juice, dill, and some salt and pepper, in another bowl. Pour the dressing over, toss to combine and serve immediately.

Nutrition Info:

- Per Serves 5g Carbs ; 15g Protein:17g Fat; 214 Calories

Sauces And Dressing Recipes

Sauces And Dressing Recipes

Keto Ranch Dip

Servings: 8
Cooking Time: 10 Minutes

Ingredients:
- 1 cup egg white, beaten
- 1 lemon juice, freshly squeezed
- Salt and pepper to taste
- 1 teaspoon mustard paste
- 1 cup olive oil
- Salt and pepper to taste

Directions:
1. Add all ingredients to a pot and bring to a simmer. Stir frequently.
2. Simmer for 10 minutes.
3. Adjust seasoning to taste.

Nutrition Info:
- Per Servings 1.2g Carbs, 3.4g Protein, 27.1g Fat, 258 Calories

Ketogenic-friendly Gravy

Servings: 6
Cooking Time: 10 Minutes

Ingredients:
- 2 tablespoons butter
- 1 white onion, chopped
- ¼ cup coconut milk
- 2 cups bone broth
- 1 tablespoon balsamic vinegar
- Salt and pepper to taste

Directions:
1. Add all ingredients to a pot and bring to a simmer. Stir frequently.
2. Simmer for 10 minutes.
3. Adjust seasoning to taste.

Nutrition Info:
- Per Servings 1.1g Carbs, 0.2g Protein, 6.3g Fat, 59 Calories

Roasted Garlic Lemon Dip

Servings: 3
Cooking Time: 30 Minutes

Ingredients:
- 3 medium lemons
- 3 cloves garlic, peeled and smashed
- 5 tablespoons olive oil, divided
- 1/2 teaspoon kosher salt
- Pepper to taste
- Salt
- Pepper

Directions:
1. Arrange a rack in the middle of the oven and heat to 400°F.
2. Cut the lemons in half crosswise and remove the seeds. Place the lemons cut-side up in a small baking dish. Add the garlic and drizzle with 2 tablespoons of the oil.
3. Roast until the lemons are tender and lightly browned, about 30 minutes. Remove the baking dish to a wire rack.
4. When the lemons are cool enough to handle, squeeze the juice into the baking dish. Discard the lemon pieces and any remaining seeds. Pour the contents of the baking dish, including the garlic, into a blender or mini food processor. Add the remaining 3 tablespoons oil and salt. Process until the garlic is completely puréed, and the sauce is emulsified and slightly thickened. Serve warm or at room temperature.

Nutrition Info:
- Per Servings 4.8g Carbs, 0.6g Protein, 17g Fat, 165 Calories

Dijon Vinaigrette

Servings: 4
Cooking Time: 5 Minutes

Ingredients:
- 2 tablespoons Dijon mustard
- Juice of ½ lemon
- 1 garlic clove, finely minced
- 1½ tablespoons red wine vinegar
- Pink Himalayan salt
- Freshly ground black pepper
- 3 tablespoons olive oil

Directions:
1. In a small bowl, whisk the mustard, lemon juice, garlic, and red wine vinegar until well combined. Season with pink Himalayan salt and pepper, and whisk again.
2. Slowly add the olive oil, a little bit at a time, whisking constantly.
3. Keep in a sealed glass container in the refrigerator for up to 1 week.

Nutrition Info:
- Per Servings 1g Carbs, 1g Protein, 11g Fat, 99 Calories

Caesar Dressing

Servings: 4
Cooking Time: 5 Minutes

Ingredients:
- ½ cup mayonnaise
- 1 tablespoon Dijon mustard
- Juice of ½ lemon
- ½ teaspoon Worcestershire sauce
- Pinch pink Himalayan salt
- Pinch freshly ground black pepper
- ¼ cup grated Parmesan cheese

Directions:
1. In a medium bowl, whisk together the mayonnaise, mustard, lemon juice, Worcestershire sauce, pink Himalayan salt, and pepper until fully combined.
2. Add the Parmesan cheese, and whisk until creamy and well blended.
3. Keep in a sealed glass container in the refrigerator for up to 1 week.

Nutrition Info:
- Per Servings Calories: 2g Carbs, 2g Protein, 23g Fat, 222 Calories

Keto Thousand Island Dressing

Servings: 10
Cooking Time: 10 Minutes

Ingredients:
- 1 cup mayonnaise
- 1 tablespoon lemon juice, freshly squeezed
- 4 tablespoons dill pickles, chopped
- 1 teaspoon Tabasco
- 1 shallot chopped finely
- Salt and pepper to taste

Directions:
1. Add all ingredients to a pot and bring to a simmer. Stir frequently.
2. Simmer for 10 minutes.
3. Adjust seasoning to taste.

Nutrition Info:
- Per Servings 2.3g Carbs, 1.7g Protein, 7.8g Fat, 85 Calories

Avocado-lime Crema

Servings: 4
Cooking Time: 5 Minutes

Ingredients:
- ½ cup sour cream
- ½ avocado
- 1 garlic clove, finely minced
- ¼ cup fresh cilantro leaves
- Juice of ½ lime
- Pinch pink Himalayan salt
- Pinch freshly ground black pepper

Directions:
1. In a food processor (or blender), mix the sour cream, avocado, garlic, cilantro, lime juice, pink Himalayan salt, and pepper until smooth and fully combined.
2. Spoon the sauce into an airtight glass jar and keep in the refrigerator for up to 3 days.

Nutrition Info:
- Per Servings Calories: 2g Carbs, 1g Protein, 8g Fat, 87 Calories

Cheesy Avocado Dip

Servings:
Cooking Time: 20 Minutes

Ingredients:
- 1/2 medium ripe avocado, peeled and pitted
- 2 crumbled blue cheese
- 1 freshly squeezed lemon juice
- 1/2 kosher salt
- 1/2 cup water

Directions:
1. Scoop the flesh of the avocado into the bowl of a food processor fitted with the blade attachment or blender.
2. Add the blue cheese, lemon juice, and salt. Blend until smooth and creamy, 30 to 40 seconds.
3. With the motor running, add the water and blend until the sauce is thinned and well-combined.

Nutrition Info:
- Per Servings 2.9g Carbs, 3.5g Protein, 7.2g Fat, 86 Calories

Celery-onion Vinaigrette

Servings: 4
Cooking Time: 0 Minutes

Ingredients:
- 1 tbsp finely chopped celery
- 1 tbsp finely chopped red onion
- 4 garlic cloves, minced
- ½ cup red wine vinegar
- 1 tbsp extra virgin olive oil

Directions:
1. Prepare the dressing by mixing pepper, celery, onion, olive oil, garlic, and vinegar in a small bowl. Whisk well to combine.
2. Let it sit for at least 30 minutes to let flavors blend.
3. Serve and enjoy with your favorite salad greens.

Nutrition Info:
- Per Servings 1.4g Carbs, 0.2g Protein, 3.4g Fat, 41 Calories

Tzatziki

Servings: 4
Cooking Time: 10 Minutes, Plus At Least 30 Minutes To Chill

Ingredients:
- ½ large English cucumber, unpeeled
- 1½ cups Greek yogurt (I use Fage)
- 2 tablespoons olive oil
- Large pinch pink Himalayan salt
- Large pinch freshly ground black pepper
- Juice of ½ lemon
- 2 garlic cloves, finely minced
- 1 tablespoon fresh dill

Directions:
1. Halve the cucumber lengthwise, and use a spoon to scoop out and discard the seeds.
2. Grate the cucumber with a zester or grater onto a large plate lined with a few layers of paper towels. Close the paper towels around the grated cucumber, and squeeze as much water out of it as you can. (This can take a while and can require multiple paper towels. You can also allow it to drain overnight in a strainer or wrapped in a few layers of cheesecloth in the fridge if you have the time.)
3. In a food processor (or blender), blend the yogurt, olive oil, pink Himalayan salt, pepper, lemon juice, and garlic until fully combined.
4. Transfer the mixture to a medium bowl, and mix in the fresh dill and grated cucumber.
5. I like to chill this sauce for at least 30 minutes before serving. Keep in a sealed glass container in the refrigerator for up to 1 week.

Nutrition Info:

- Per Servings 5g Carbs, 8g Protein, 11g Fat, 149 Calories

Caesar Salad Dressing

Servings: 6
Cooking Time: 10 Minutes

Ingredients:
- ½ cup olive oil
- 1 tablespoon Dijon mustard
- ½ cup parmesan cheese, grated
- 2/3-ounce anchovies, chopped
- ½ lemon juice, freshly squeezed
- Salt and pepper to taste

Directions:
1. Add all ingredients to a pot and bring to a simmer. Stir frequently.
2. Simmer for 10 minutes.
3. Adjust seasoning to taste.

Nutrition Info:
- Per Servings 1.5g Carbs, 3.4g Protein, 20.7g Fat, 203 Calories

Green Jalapeno Sauce

Servings: 1
Cooking Time: 0 Minutes

Ingredients:
- ½ avocado
- 1 large jalapeno
- 1 cup fresh cilantro
- 2 tablespoons extra virgin olive oil
- 3 tablespoons water
- Water
- ½ teaspoon salt

Directions:
1. Add all ingredients in a blender.
2. Blend until smooth and creamy.
3. Serve and enjoy.

Nutrition Info:
- Per Servings 10g Carbs, 2.4g Protein, 42g Fat, 407 Calories

Feta Avocado Dip

Servings: 4
Cooking Time: 0 Minutes

Ingredients:
- 2 avocadoes (mashed)
- ½ cup feta cheese (crumbled)
- 1 plum tomatoes (diced)
- 1 teaspoon garlic (minced)
- ½ lemon (juiced)
- Salt
- Pepper
- 4 tablespoons olive oil

Directions:
1. Fold ingredients together. Do not stir too much to leave chunks of feta and avocado.
2. Serve and enjoy.

Nutrition Info:
- Per Servings 8.1g Carbs, 5g Protein, 19g Fat, 220 Calories

Vegetarian Fish Sauce

Servings: 16
Cooking Time: 20 Minutes

Ingredients:
- 1/4 cup dried shiitake mushrooms
- 1-2 tbsp tamari (for a depth of flavor)
- 3 tbsp coconut aminos
- 1 ¼ cup water
- 2 tsp sea salt

Directions:
1. To a small saucepan, add water, coconut aminos, dried shiitake mushrooms, and sea salt. Bring to a boil, then cover, reduce heat, and simmer for 15-20 minutes.
2. Remove from heat and let cool slightly. Pour liquid through a fine-mesh strainer into a bowl, pressing on the mushroom mixture with a spoon to squeeze out any remaining liquid.
3. To the bowl, add tamari. Taste and adjust as needed, adding more sea salt for saltiness.
4. Store in a sealed container in the refrigerator for up to 1 month and shake well before use. Or pour into an ice cube tray, freeze, and store in a freezer-safe container for up to 2 months.

Nutrition Info:
- Per Servings 5g Carbs, 0.3g Protein, 2g Fat, 39.1 Calories

Cowboy Sauce

Servings: 6
Cooking Time: 10 Minutes

Ingredients:
- 1 stick butter
- 2 cloves of garlic, minced
- 1 tablespoon fresh horseradish, grated
- 1 teaspoon dried thyme
- 1 teaspoon paprika powder
- Salt and pepper to taste
- ¼ cup water

Directions:
1. Add all ingredients to a pot and bring to a simmer.
2. Simmer for 10 minutes.
3. Adjust seasoning to taste.

Nutrition Info:
- Per Servings 0.9g Carbs, 1.3g Protein, 20.6g Fat, 194 Calories

Simple Tomato Sauce

Servings: 4
Cooking Time: 20 Minutes

Ingredients:
- 1 can whole peeled tomatoes
- 3 garlic cloves, smashed
- 5 tablespoons olive oil
- Kosher salt
- 2 tablespoons unsalted butter
- Salt

Directions:
1. Purée tomatoes in a food processor until they're as smooth or chunky as you like.
2. Transfer tomatoes to a large Dutch oven or other heavy pot. (Or, use an immersion blender and blend directly in the pot.)
3. Add garlic, oil, and a 5-finger pinch of salt.
4. Bring to a boil and cook, occasionally stirring, until sauce is reduced by about one-third, about 20 minutes. Stir in butter.

Nutrition Info:
- Per Servings 7.6g Carbs, 1.9g Protein, 21.3g Fat, 219 Calories

Peanut Sauce

Servings: 4
Cooking Time: 5 Minutes

Ingredients:
- ½ cup creamy peanut butter (I use Justin's)
- 2 tablespoons soy sauce (or coconut aminos)
- 1 teaspoon Sriracha sauce
- 1 teaspoon toasted sesame oil
- 1 teaspoon garlic powder

Directions:
1. In a food processor (or blender), blend the peanut butter, soy sauce, Sriracha sauce, sesame oil, and garlic powder until thoroughly mixed.
2. Pour into an airtight glass container and keep in the refrigerator for up to 1 week.

Nutrition Info:
- Per Servings Calories: 185; Total Fat: 15g; Carbs: 8g; Net Carbs: 6g; Fiber: 2g; Protein: 7g

Alfredo Sauce

Servings: 2
Cooking Time: 10 Minutes

Ingredients:
- 4 tablespoons butter
- 2 ounces cream cheese
- 1 cup heavy (whipping) cream
- ½ cup grated Parmesan cheese
- 1 garlic clove, finely minced
- 1 teaspoon dried Italian seasoning
- Pink Himalayan salt
- Freshly ground black pepper

Directions:
1. In a heavy medium saucepan over medium heat, combine the butter, cream cheese, and heavy cream. Whisk slowly and constantly until the butter and cream cheese melt.
2. Add the Parmesan, garlic, and Italian seasoning. Continue to whisk until everything is well blended. Turn the heat to medium-low and simmer, stirring occasionally, for 5 to 8 minutes to allow the sauce to blend and thicken.
3. Season with pink Himalayan salt and pepper, and stir to combine.
4. Toss with your favorite hot, precooked, keto-friendly noodles and serve.
5. Keep this sauce in a sealed glass container in the refrigerator for up to 4 days.

Nutrition Info:
- Per Servings 2g Carbs, 5g Protein, 30g Fat, 294 Calories

Artichoke Pesto Dip

Servings: 1
Cooking Time: 20 Minutes

Ingredients:
- 1 jar marinated artichoke hearts
- 8 ounces cream cheese (at room temperature)
- 4 ounces parmesan cheese (grated)
- 2 tablespoons basil pesto
- ¼ cup shelled pistachio (chopped, optional)

Directions:
1. Preheat oven to 375oF.
2. Drain and chop artichoke hearts.
3. Mix artichokes, cream cheese, parmesan, and pesto.
4. Pour into 4 ramekins evenly.
5. Bake for 15-20 minutes.

Nutrition Info:
- Per Servings 5g Carbs, 8g Protein, 19g Fat, 214 Calories

Fat-burning Dressing

Servings: 6
Cooking Time: 3 Minutes

Ingredients:
- 2 tablespoons coconut oil
- ¼ cup olive oil
- 2 cloves of garlic, minced
- 2 tablespoons freshly chopped herbs of your choice
- ¼ cup mayonnaise
- Salt and pepper to taste

Directions:
1. Heat the coconut oil and olive oil and sauté the garlic until fragrant in a saucepan.
2. Allow cooling slightly before adding the mayonnaise.
3. Season with salt and pepper to taste.

Nutrition Info:
- Per Servings 0.6g Carbs, 14.1g Protein, 22.5g Fat, 262 Calories

Green Goddess Dressing

Servings: 4
Cooking Time: 5 Minutes

Ingredients:
- 2 tablespoon buttermilk
- ¼ cup Greek yogurt
- 1 teaspoon apple cider vinegar
- 1 garlic clove, minced
- 1 tablespoon olive oil
- 1 tablespoon fresh parsley leaves

Directions:
1. In a food processor (or blender), combine the buttermilk, yogurt, apple cider vinegar, garlic, olive oil, and parsley. Blend until fully combined.
2. Pour into a sealed glass container and chill in the refrigerator for at least 30 minutes before serving. This dressing will keep in the fridge for up to 1 week.

Nutrition Info:
- Per Servings 1g Carbs, 1g Protein, 6g Fat, 62 Calories

Garlic Aioli

Servings: 4
Cooking Time: 5 Minutes, Plus 30 Minutes To Chill

Ingredients:
- ½ cup mayonnaise
- 2 garlic cloves, minced
- Juice of 1 lemon
- 1 tablespoon chopped fresh flat-leaf Italian parsley
- 1 teaspoon chopped chives
- Pink Himalayan salt
- Freshly ground black pepper

Directions:
1. In a food processor (or blender), combine the mayonnaise, garlic, lemon juice, parsley, and chives, and season with pink Himalayan salt and pepper. Blend until fully combined.
2. Pour into a sealed glass container and chill in the refrigerator for at least 30 minutes before serving. (This sauce will keep in the fridge for up to 1 week.)

Nutrition Info:
- Per Servings Calories: 3g Carbs, 1g Protein, 22g Fat, 204 Calories

Sriracha Mayo

Servings: 4
Cooking Time: 5 Minutes

Ingredients:
- ½ cup mayonnaise
- 2 tablespoons Sriracha sauce
- ½ teaspoon garlic powder
- ½ teaspoon onion powder
- ¼ teaspoon paprika

Directions:
1. In a small bowl, whisk together the mayonnaise, Sriracha, garlic powder, onion powder, and paprika until well mixed.
2. Pour into an airtight glass container, and keep in the refrigerator for up to 1 week.

Nutrition Info:
- Per Servings Calories: 2g Carbs, 1g Protein, 22g Fat, 201 Calories

Lemon Tahini Sauce

Servings: 2
Cooking Time: 5 Minutes

Ingredients:
- 1/2 cup packed fresh herbs, such as parsley, basil, mint, cilantro, dill, or chives
- 1/4 cup tahini
- Juice of 1 lemon
- 1/2 teaspoon kosher salt
- 1 tablespoon water

Directions:
1. Place all the ingredients in the bowl of a food processor fitted with the blade attachment or a blender. Process continuously until the herbs are finely minced, and the sauce is well-blended, 3 to 4 minutes.
2. Serve immediately or store in a covered container in the refrigerator until ready to serve.

Nutrition Info:
- Per Servings 4.3g Carbs, 2.8g Protein, 8.1g Fat, 94 Calories

Chunky Blue Cheese Dressing

Servings: 4
Cooking Time: 5 Minutes

Ingredients:
- ½ cup sour cream
- ½ cup mayonnaise
- Juice of ½ lemon
- ½ teaspoon Worcestershire sauce
- Pink Himalayan salt
- Freshly ground black pepper
- 2 ounces crumbled blue cheese

Directions:
1. In a medium bowl, whisk the sour cream, mayonnaise, lemon juice, and Worcestershire sauce. Season with pink Himalayan salt and pepper, and whisk again until fully combined.
2. Fold in the crumbled blue cheese until well combined.
3. Keep in a sealed glass container in the refrigerator for up to 1 week.

Nutrition Info:
- Per Servings 3g Carbs, 7g Protein, 32g Fat, 306 Calories

Buttery Dijon Sauce

Servings: 2
Cooking Time: 0 Minutes

Ingredients:
- 3 parts brown butter
- 1-part vinegar or citrus juice or a combo
- 1-part strong Dijon mustard
- A small handful of flat-leaf parsley (optional)
- 3/4 teaspoon freshly ground pepper
- 1 teaspoon salt

Directions:
1. Add everything to a food processor and blitz until just smooth.
2. You can also mix this up with an immersion blender. Use immediately or store in the refrigerator for up to one day. Blend again before use.

Nutrition Info:
- Per Servings 0.7g Carbs, 0.4g Protein, 34.4g Fat, 306 Calories

Buffalo Sauce

Servings: 8
Cooking Time: 30 Minutes

Ingredients:
- 8 ounces Cream Cheese (softened)
- ½ cup Buffalo Wing Sauce
- ½ cup Blue Cheese Dressing
- 1 ½ cups Cheddar Cheese (Shredded)

- 1 ¼ cups Chicken Breast (Cooked)

Directions:
1. Preheat oven to 350oF.
2. Blend together buffalo sauce, white salad dressing, cream cheese, chicken, and shredded cheese.
3. Top with any other optional ingredients like blue cheese chunks.
4. Bake for 25-30 minutes

Nutrition Info:
- Per Servings 2.2g Carbs, 16g Protein, 28g Fat, 325 Calories

Avocado Mayo

Servings: 4
Cooking Time: 5 Minutes

Ingredients:
- 1 medium avocado, cut into chunks
- ½ teaspoon ground cayenne pepper
- Juice of ½ lime
- 2 tablespoons fresh cilantro leaves (optional)
- Pinch pink Himalayan salt
- ¼ cup olive oil

Directions:
1. In a food processor (or blender), blend the avocado, cayenne pepper, lime juice, cilantro, and pink Himalayan salt until all the ingredients are well combined and smooth.
2. Slowly incorporate the olive oil, adding 1 tablespoon at a time, pulsing the food processor in between.
3. Keep in a sealed glass container in the refrigerator for up to 1 week.

Nutrition Info:
- Per Servings 1g Carbs, 1g Protein, 5g Fat, 58 Calories

Greek Yogurt Dressing

Servings: 2
Cooking Time: 0 Minutes

Ingredients:
- ¼ tsp ground ginger
- ½ tsp prepared mustard
- 2 tbsp low-fat mayonnaise
- ½ cup plain Greek yogurt
- Salt and pepper to taste

Directions:
1. In a bowl, whisk well all ingredients.
2. Adjust seasoning to taste.
3. Serve and enjoy with your favorite salad greens.

Nutrition Info:
- Per Servings 3.5g Carbs, 3.0g Protein, 2.8g Fat, 51 Calories

Desserts And Drinks Recipes

Desserts And Drinks Recipes

Ice Cream Bars Covered With Chocolate

Servings: 15
Cooking Time: 4 Hours And 20 Minutes

Ingredients:
- Ice Cream:
- 1 cup heavy whipping cream
- 1 tsp vanilla extract
- ¾ tsp xanthan gum
- ½ cup peanut butter
- 1 cup half and half
- 1 ½ cups almond milk
- ⅓ tsp stevia powder
- 1 tbsp vegetable glycerin
- 3 tbsp xylitol
- Chocolate:
- ¾ cup coconut oil
- ¼ cup cocoa butter pieces, chopped
- 2 ounces unsweetened chocolate
- 3 ½ tsp THM super sweet blend

Directions:
1. Blend all ice cream ingredients until smooth. Place in an ice cream maker and follow the instructions. Spread the ice cream into a lined pan, and freezer for about 4 hours.
2. Combine all chocolate ingredients in a microwave-safe bowl and heat until melted. Allow cooling. Remove the ice cream from the freezer and slice into bars. Dip them into the cooled chocolate mixture and return to the freezer for about 10 minutes before serving.

Nutrition Info:
- Per Servings 5g Carbs, 4g Protein, 32g Fat, 345 Calories

Cranberry White Chocolate Barks

Servings: 6
Cooking Time: 5 Minutes

Ingredients:
- 10 oz unsweetened white chocolate, chopped
- ½ cup erythritol
- ⅓ cup dried cranberries, chopped
- ⅓ cup toasted walnuts, chopped
- ¼ tsp pink salt

Directions:
1. Line a baking sheet with parchment paper. Pour chocolate and erythritol in a bowl, and melt in the microwave for 25 seconds, stirring three times until fully melted. Stir in the cranberries, walnuts, and salt, reserving a few cranberries and walnuts for garnishing.
2. Pour the mixture on the baking sheet and spread out. Sprinkle with remaining cranberries and walnuts. Refrigerate for 2 hours to set. Break into bite-size pieces to serve.

Nutrition Info:
- Per Servings 3g Carbs, 6g Protein, 21g Fat, 225 Calories

Chocolate Marshmallows

Servings: 4
Cooking Time: 30 Minutes

Ingredients:
- 2 tbsp unsweetened cocoa powder
- ½ tsp vanilla extract
- ½ cup swerve
- 1 tbsp xanthan gum mixed in 1 tbsp water
- A pinch Salt
- 6 tbsp Cool water
- 2 ½ tsp Gelatin powder
- Dusting:
- 1 tbsp unsweetened cocoa powder
- 1 tbsp swerve confectioner's sugar

Directions:
1. Line the loaf pan with parchment paper and grease with cooking spray; set aside. In a saucepan, mix the swerve, 2 tbsp of water, xanthan gum mixture, and salt. Place the pan over medium heat and bring to a boil. Insert the thermometer and let the ingredients simmer to 238 F, for 7 minutes.
2. In a small bowl, add 2 tbsp of water and sprinkle the gelatin on top. Let sit there without stirring to dissolve for 5 minutes. While the gelatin dissolves, pour the remaining water in a small bowl and heat in the microwave for 30 seconds. Stir in cocoa powder and mix it into the gelatin.
3. When the sugar solution has hit the right temperature, gradually pour it directly into the gelatin mixture while continuously whisking. Beat for 10 minutes to get a light and fluffy consistency.
4. Next, stir in the vanilla and pour the blend into the loaf pan. Let the marshmallows set for 3 hours and then use an oiled knife to cut it into cubes; place them on a plate. Mix the remaining cocoa powder and confectioner's sugar together. Sift it over the marshmallows.

Nutrition Info:
- Per Servings 5.1g Carbs, 0.5g Protein, 2.2g Fat, 55 Calories

Walnut Cookies

Servings: 12
Cooking Time: 25 Minutes

Ingredients:
- 1 egg
- 2 cups ground pecans
- ¼ cup sweetener
- ½ tsp baking soda
- 1 tbsp butter
- 20 walnuts halves

Directions:
1. Preheat the oven to 350ºF. Mix the ingredients, except the walnuts, until combined. Make 20 balls out of the mixture and press them with your thumb onto a lined cookie sheet. Top each cookie with a walnut half. Bake for about 12 minutes.

Nutrition Info:
- Per Servings 0.6g Carbs, 1.6g Protein, 11g Fat, 101 Calories

Green And Fruity Smoothie

Servings: 2
Cooking Time: 0 Minutes

Ingredients:
- 1 cup spinach, packed
- ½ cup strawberries, chopped
- ½ avocado, peeled, pitted, and frozen
- 1 tbsp almond butter
- ¼ cup packed kale, stem discarded, and leaves chopped
- 1 cup ice-cold water
- 5 tablespoons MCT oil or coconut oil

Directions:
1. Blend all ingredients in a blender until smooth and creamy.
2. Serve and enjoy.

Nutrition Info:
- Per Servings 10g Carbs, 1.6g Protein, 47.3g Fat, 459 Calories

Chocolate Chip Cookies

Servings: 4
Cooking Time: 20 Minutes

Ingredients:
- 1 cup butter, softened
- 2 cups swerve brown sugar
- 3 eggs
- 2 cups almond flour
- 2 cups unsweetened chocolate chips

Directions:
1. Preheat oven to 350ºF and line a baking sheet with parchment paper.
2. Whisk the butter and sugar with a hand mixer for 3 minutes or until light and fluffy. Add the eggs one at a time, and scrape the sides as you whisk. Mix in the almond flour in low speed until well combined.
3. Fold in the chocolate chips. Scoop 3 tablespoons each on the baking sheet creating spaces between each mound and bake for 15 minutes to swell and harden. Remove, cool and serve.

Nutrition Info:
- Per Servings 8.9g Carbs, 6.3g Protein, 27g Fat, 317 Calories

Lettuce Green Shake

Servings: 1
Cooking Time: 0 Minutes

Ingredients:
- ¾ cup whole milk yogurt
- 2 cups 5-lettuce mix salad greens
- 3 tbsp MCT oil
- 1 tbsp chia seeds
- 1 ½ cups water
- 1 packet Stevia, or more to taste

Directions:
1. Add all ingredients in a blender.
2. Blend until smooth and creamy.
3. Serve and enjoy.

Nutrition Info:
- Per Servings 6.1g Carbs, 8.1g Protein, 47g Fat, 483 Calories

Strawberry And Basil Lemonade

Servings: 4
Cooking Time: 3 Minutes

Ingredients:
- 4 cups water
- 12 strawberries, leaves removed
- 1 cup fresh lemon juice
- ⅓ cup fresh basil
- ¾ cup swerve
- Crushed Ice
- Halved strawberries to garnish
- Basil leaves to garnish

Directions:
1. Spoon some ice into 4 serving glasses and set aside. In a pitcher, add the water, strawberries, lemon juice, basil, and swerve. Insert the blender and process the ingredients for 30 seconds.
2. The mixture should be pink and the basil finely chopped. Adjust the taste and add the ice in the glasses. Drop 2 strawberry halves and some basil in each glass and serve immediately.

Nutrition Info:
- Per Servings 5.8g Carbs, 0.7g Protein, 0.1g Fat, 66 Calories

Berry Tart

Servings: 4
Cooking Time: 45 Minutes

Ingredients:
- 4 eggs
- 2 tsp coconut oil
- 2 cups berries
- 1 cup coconut milk
- 1 cup almond flour
- ¼ cup sweetener
- ½ tsp vanilla powder
- 1 tbsp powdered sweetener
- A pinch of salt

Directions:
1. Preheat the oven to 350ºF. Place all ingredients except coconut oil, berries, and powdered sweetener, in a blender; blend until smooth. Gently fold in the berries. Grease a baking dish with the oil. Pour the mixture into the prepared pan and bake for 35 minutes. Sprinkle with powdered sugar to serve.

Nutrition Info:
- Per Servings 4.9g Carbs, 15g Protein, 26.5g Fat, 305 Calories

Strawberry Yogurt Shake

Servings: 1
Cooking Time: 0 Minutes

Ingredients:
- ½ cup whole milk yogurt
- 4 strawberries, chopped
- 1 tbsp cocoa powder
- 3 tbsp coconut oil
- 1 tbsp pepitas
- 1 ½ cups water
- 1 packet Stevia, or more to taste

Directions:
1. Add all ingredients in a blender.
2. Blend until smooth and creamy.
3. Serve and enjoy.

Nutrition Info:
- Per Servings 10.5g Carbs, 7.7g Protein, 49.3g Fat, 496 Calories

Nutty Arugula Yogurt Smoothie

Servings: 1
Cooking Time: 0 Minutes

Ingredients:
- 1 cup whole milk yogurt
- 1 cup baby arugula
- 3 tbsps avocado oil
- 2 tbsps macadamia nuts
- 1 packet Stevia, or more to taste
- 1 cup water

Directions:
1. Add all ingredients in a blender.
2. Blend until smooth and creamy.
3. Serve and enjoy.

Nutrition Info:
- Per Servings 9.4g Carbs, 9.3g Protein, 51.5g Fat, 540 Calories

Five Greens Smoothie

Servings: 4
Cooking Time: 5 Minutes

Ingredients:
- 6 kale leaves, chopped
- 3 stalks celery, chopped
- 1 ripe avocado, skinned, pitted, sliced
- 1 cup ice cubes
- 2 cups spinach, chopped
- 1 large cucumber, peeled and chopped
- Chia seeds to garnish

Directions:
1. In a blender, add the kale, celery, avocado, and ice cubes, and blend for 45 seconds. Add the spinach and cucumber, and process for another 45 seconds until smooth.
2. Pour the smoothie into glasses, garnish with chia seeds and serve the drink immediately.

Nutrition Info:
- Per Servings 2.9g Carbs, 3.2g Protein, 7.8g Fat, 124 Calories

Strawberry-coconut Shake

Servings: 1
Cooking Time: 0 Minutes

Ingredients:
- ½ cup whole milk yogurt
- 3 tbsp MCT oil
- ¼ cup strawberries, chopped
- 1 tbsp coconut flakes, unsweetened
- 1 tbsp hemp seeds
- 1 ½ cups water
- 1 packet Stevia, or more to taste

Directions:
1. Add all ingredients in a blender.
2. Blend until smooth and creamy.
3. Serve and enjoy.

Nutrition Info:
- Per Servings 10.2g Carbs, 6.4g Protein, 50.9g Fat, 511 Calories

Passion Fruit Cheesecake Slices

Servings: 8
Cooking Time: 2 Hours 30 Minutes

Ingredients:
- 1 cup crushed almond biscuits
- ½ cup melted butter
- Filling:
- 1 ½ cups cream cheese
- ¾ cup swerve
- 1 ½ whipping cream
- 1 tsp vanilla bean paste
- 4-6 tbsp cold water
- 1 tbsp gelatin powder
- Passionfruit Jelly
- 1 cup passion fruit pulp
- ¼ cup swerve confectioner's sugar
- 1 tsp gelatin powder
- ¼ cup water, room temperature

Directions:
1. Mix the crushed biscuits and butter in a bowl, spoon into a spring-form pan, and use the back of the spoon to level at the bottom. Set aside in the fridge. Put the cream cheese, swerve, and vanilla paste into a bowl, and use the hand mixer to whisk until smooth; set aside.
2. In a bowl, add 2 tbsp of cold water and sprinkle 1 tbsp of gelatin powder. Let dissolve for 5 minutes. Pour the gelatin liquid along with the whipping cream in the cheese mixture and fold gently.
3. Remove the spring-form pan from the refrigerator and pour over the mixture. Return to the fridge.
4. Repeat the dissolving process for the remaining gelatin and once your out of ingredients, pour the confectioner's sugar, and ¼ cup of water into it. Mix and stir in the passion fruit pulp.
5. Remove the cake again and pour the jelly over it. Swirl the pan to make the jelly level up. Place the pan back into the fridge to cool for 2 hours. When completely set, remove and unlock the spring-pan. Lift the pan from the cake and slice the dessert.

Nutrition Info:
- Per Servings 6.1g Carbs, 4.4g Protein, 18g Fat, 287 Calories

Green Tea Brownies With Macadamia Nuts

Servings: 4
Cooking Time: 28 Minutes

Ingredients:
- 1 tbsp green tea powder
- ¼ cup unsalted butter, melted
- 4 tbsp swerve confectioner's sugar
- A pinch of salt
- ¼ cup coconut flour
- ½ tsp low carb baking powder
- 1 egg
- ¼ cup chopped macadamia nuts

Directions:
1. Preheat the oven to 350ºF and line a square baking dish with parchment paper. Pour the melted butter into a bowl, add sugar and salt, and whisk to combine. Crack the egg into the bowl.
2. Beat the mixture until the egg has incorporated. Pour the coconut flour, green tea, and baking powder into a fine-mesh sieve and sift them into the egg bowl; stir. Add the nuts, stir again, and pour the mixture into the lined baking dish. Bake for 18 minutes, remove and slice into brownie cubes. Serve warm.

Nutrition Info:
- Per Servings 2.2g Carbs, 5.2g Protein, 23.1g Fat, 248 Calories

Granny Smith Apple Tart

Servings: 8
Cooking Time: 65 Minutes

Ingredients:
- 6 tbsp butter
- 2 cups almond flour
- 1 tsp cinnamon
- ⅓ cup sweetener
- Filling:
- 2 cups sliced Granny Smith
- ¼ cup butter
- ¼ cup sweetener
- ½ tsp cinnamon
- ½ tsp lemon juice
- Topping:
- ¼ tsp cinnamon
- 2 tbsp sweetener

Directions:
1. Preheat your oven to 370ºF and combine all crust ingredients in a bowl. Press this mixture into the bottom of a greased pan. Bake for 5 minutes.
2. Meanwhile, combine the apples and lemon juice in a bowl and let them sit until the crust is ready. Arrange them on top of the crust. Combine the rest of the filling ingredients, and brush this mixture over the apples. Bake for about 30 minutes.
3. Press the apples down with a spatula, return to oven, and bake for 20 more minutes. Combine the cinnamon and sweetener, in a bowl, and sprinkle over the tart.
4. Note: Granny Smith apples have just 9.5g of net carbs per 100g. Still high for you? Substitute with Chayote squash, which has the same texture and rich nutrients, and just around 4g of net carbs .

Nutrition Info:
- Per Servings 6.7g Carbs, 7g Protein, 26g Fat, 302 Calories

Mixed Berry Nuts Mascarpone Bowl

Servings: 4
Cooking Time: 8 Minutes

Ingredients:
- 4 cups Greek yogurt
- liquid stevia to taste
- 1 ½ cups mascarpone cheese
- 1 ½ cups blueberries and raspberries
- 1 cup toasted pecans

Directions:
1. Mix the yogurt, stevia, and mascarpone in a bowl until evenly combined. Divide the mixture into 4 bowls, share the berries and pecans on top of the cream. Serve the dessert immediately.

Nutrition Info:
- Per Servings 5g Carbs, 20g Protein, 40g Fat, 480 Calories

Strawberry-choco Shake

Servings: 1
Cooking Time: 0 Minutes

Ingredients:
- ½ cup heavy cream, liquid
- 1 tbsp cocoa powder
- 1 packet Stevia, or more to taste
- 4 strawberries, sliced
- 1 tbsp coconut flakes, unsweetened
- 1 ½ cups water
- 3 tbsps coconut oil

Directions:
1. Add all ingredients in a blender.
2. Blend until smooth and creamy.
3. Serve and enjoy.

Nutrition Info:
- Per Servings 10.1g Carbs, 2.6g Protein, 65.3g Fat, 610 Calories

Vanilla Chocolate Mousse

Servings: 4
Cooking Time: 30 Minutes

Ingredients:
- 3 eggs
- 1 cup dark chocolate chips
- 1 cup heavy cream
- 1 cup fresh strawberries, sliced
- 1 vanilla extract
- 1 tbsp swerve

Directions:
1. Melt the chocolate in a bowl, in your microwave for a minute on high, and let it cool for 10 minutes.
2. Meanwhile, in a medium-sized mixing bowl, whip the cream until very soft. Add the eggs, vanilla extract, and swerve; whisk to combine. Fold int the cooled chocolate.
3. Divide the mousse between four glasses, top with the strawberry slices and chill in the fridge for at least 30 minutes before serving.

Nutrition Info:
- Per Servings 3.7g Carbs, 7.6g Protein, 25g Fat, 370 Calories

Creamy Choco Shake

Servings: 1
Cooking Time: 0 Minutes

Ingredients:
- ½ cup heavy cream
- 2 tbsp cocoa powder
- 1 packet Stevia, or more to taste
- 1 cup water
- 3 tbsps coconut oil

Directions:
1. Add all ingredients in a blender.
2. Blend until smooth and creamy.
3. Serve and enjoy.

Nutrition Info:
- Per Servings 7.9g Carbs, 3.2g Protein, 64.6g Fat, 582 Calories

Cinnamon And Turmeric Latte

Servings: 4
Cooking Time: 7 Minutes

Ingredients:
- 3 cups almond milk
- ⅓ tsp cinnamon powder
- 1 cup brewed coffee
- ½ tsp turmeric powder
- 1 ½ tsp erythritol
- Cinnamon sticks to garnish

Directions:
1. In the blender, add the almond milk, cinnamon powder, coffee, turmeric, and erythritol. Blend the ingredients at medium speed for 45 seconds and pour the mixture into a saucepan.
2. Set the pan over low heat and heat through for 5 minutes; do not boil. Keep swirling the pan to prevent from boiling. Turn the heat off, and serve in latte cups, with a cinnamon stick in each one.

Nutrition Info:
- Per Servings 0.3g Carbs, 3.9g Protein, 12g Fat, 132 Calories

Coconut Cheesecake

Servings: 12
Cooking Time: 4 Hours And 50 Minutes

Ingredients:
- Crust
- 2 egg whites
- ¼ cup erythritol
- 3 cups desiccated coconut
- 1 tsp coconut oil
- ¼ cup melted butter
- Filling:
- 3 tbsp lemon juice
- 6 ounces raspberries
- 2 cups erythritol
- 1 cup whipped cream
- Zest of 1 lemon
- 24 ounces cream cheese

Directions:
1. Apply the coconut oil to the bottom and sides of a springform pan. Line with parchment paper. Preheat your oven to 350ºF and mix all crust ingredients. Pour the crust into the pan.
2. Bake for about 25 minutes; then let cool.
3. Meanwhile, beat the cream cheese with an electric mixer until soft. Add the lemon juice, zest, and erythritol.
4. Fold the whipped cream into the cheese cream mixture. Fold in the raspberries gently. Spoon the filling into the baked and cooled crust. Place in the fridge for 4 hours.

Nutrition Info:
- Per Servings 3g Carbs, 5g Protein, 25g Fat, 256 Calories

Chocolate Bark With Almonds

Servings: 12
Cooking Time: 1 Hour 15 Minutes

Ingredients:
- ½ cup toasted almonds, chopped
- ½ cup butter
- 10 drops stevia
- ¼ tsp salt
- ½ cup unsweetened coconut flakes
- 4 ounces dark chocolate

Directions:
1. Melt together the butter and chocolate, in the microwave, for 90 seconds. Remove and stir in stevia.
2. Line a cookie sheet with waxed paper and spread the chocolate evenly. Scatter the almonds on top, coconut flakes, and sprinkle with salt. Refrigerate for one hour.

Nutrition Info:
- Per Servings 1.9g Carbs, 1.9g Protein, 15.3g Fat, 161 Calories

Raspberry Nut Truffles

Servings: 4
Cooking Time: 6 Minutes + Cooling Time

Ingredients:
- 2 cups raw cashews
- 2 tbsp flax seed
- 1 ½ cups sugar-free raspberry preserves
- 3 tbsp swerve
- 10 oz unsweetened chocolate chips
- 3 tbsp olive oil

Directions:
1. Line a baking sheet with parchment paper and set aside. Grind the cashews and flax seeds in a blender for 45 seconds until smoothly crushed; add the raspberry and 2 tbsp of swerve.
2. Process further for 1 minute until well combined. Form 1-inch balls of the mixture, place on the baking sheet, and freeze for 1 hour or until firmed up.
3. Melt the chocolate chips, oil, and 1tbsp of swerve in a microwave for 1 ½ minutes. Toss the truffles to coat in the chocolate mixture, put on the baking sheet, and freeze further for at least 2 hours.

Nutrition Info:
- Per Servings 3.5g Carbs, 12g Protein, 18.3g Fat, 251 Calories

Nutritiously Green Milk Shake

Servings: 1
Cooking Time: 5 Minutes

Ingredients:
- 1 cup coconut cream
- 1 packet Stevia, or more to taste
- 1 tbsp coconut flakes, unsweetened
- 2 cups spring mix salad
- 3 tbsps coconut oil
- 1 cup water

Directions:
1. Add all ingredients in a blender.
2. Blend until smooth and creamy.
3. Serve and enjoy.

Nutrition Info:
- Per Servings 10g Carbs, 10.5g Protein, 95.3g Fat, 887 Calories

Blackberry-chocolate Shake

Servings: 1
Cooking Time: 0 Minutes

Ingredients:
- ½ cup half and half
- 1 tbsp blackberries
- 3 tbsps MCT oil
- 1 tbsp Dutch-processed cocoa powder
- 2 tbsp Macadamia nuts, chopped
- 1 ½ cups water
- 1 packet Stevia, or more to taste

Directions:
1. Add all ingredients in a blender.
2. Blend until smooth and creamy.
3. Serve and enjoy.

Nutrition Info:
- Per Servings 10.1g Carbs, 2.7g Protein, 43.9g Fat, 463 Calories

Blackcurrant Iced Tea

Servings: 4
Cooking Time: 8 Minutes

Ingredients:
- 6 unflavored tea bags
- 2 cups water
- ½ cup sugar-free blackcurrant extract
- Swerve to taste
- Ice cubes for serving
- Lemon slices to garnish, cut on the side

Directions:
1. Pour the ice cubes in a pitcher and place it in the fridge.
2. Bring the water to boil in a saucepan over medium heat

for 3 minutes and turn the heat off. Stir in the sugar to dissolve and steep the tea bags in the water for 2 minutes.
3. Remove the bags after and let the tea cool down. Stir in the blackcurrant extract until well incorporated, remove the pitcher from the fridge, and pour the mixture over the ice cubes.
4. Let sit for 3 minutes to cool and after, pour the mixture into tall glasses. Add some more ice cubes, place the lemon slices on the rim of the glasses, and serve the tea cold.

Nutrition Info:
- Per Servings 5g Carbs, 0g Protein, 0g Fat, 22 Calories

Smarties Cookies

Servings: 8
Cooking Time: 10 Mins

Ingredients:
- 1/4 cup. butter
- 1/2 cup. almond flour
- 1 tsp. vanilla essence
- 12 oz. bag of smarties
- 1 cup. stevia
- 1/4 tsp. baking powder

Directions:
1. Sift in flour and baking powder in a bowl, then stir through butter and mix until well combined.
2. Whisk in stevia and vanilla essence , stir until thick.
3. Then add the smarties and use your hand to mix and divide into small balls.
4. Bake until completely cooked, about 10 minutes. Let it cool and serve.

Nutrition Info:
- Per Servings 20.77g Carbs, 3.7g Protein, 11.89g Fat, 239 Calories

Baby Kale And Yogurt Smoothie

Servings: 1
Cooking Time: 0 Minutes

Ingredients:
- ½ cup whole milk yogurt
- ½ cup baby kale greens
- 1 packet Stevia, or more to taste
- 3 tbsps MCT oil
- ½ tbsp sunflower seeds
- 1 cup water

Directions:
1. Add all ingredients in a blender.
2. Blend until smooth and creamy.
3. Serve and enjoy.

Nutrition Info:
- Per Servings 2.6g Carbs, 11.0g Protein, 26.2g Fat, 329 Calories

Lemon Cheesecake Mousse

Servings: 4
Cooking Time: 5 Minutes +cooling Time

Ingredients:
- 24 oz cream cheese, softened
- 2 cups swerve confectioner's sugar
- 2 lemons, juiced and zested
- Pink salt to taste
- 1 cup whipped cream + extra for garnish

Directions:
1. Whip the cream cheese in a bowl with a hand mixer until light and fluffy. Mix in the sugar, lemon juice, and salt. Fold in the whipped cream to evenly combine.
2. Spoon the mousse into serving cups and refrigerate to thicken for 1 hour. Swirl with extra whipped cream and garnish lightly with lemon zest. Serve immediately.

Nutrition Info:
- Per Servings 3g Carbs, 12g Protein, 18g Fat, 223 Calories

No Bake Lemon Cheese-stard

Servings: 8
Cooking Time: 0 Minutes

Ingredients:
- 1 tsp vanilla flavoring
- 1 tbsp lemon juice
- 2 oz heavy cream
- 8 oz softened cream cheese
- 1 tsp liquid low carb sweetener (Splenda)
- 1 tsp stevia

Directions:
1. Mix all ingredients in a large mixing bowl until the mixture has a pudding consistency.
2. Pour the mixture to small serving cups and refrigerate for a few hours until it sets.
3. Serve chilled.

Nutrition Info:
- Per Servings 1.4g Carbs, 2.2g Protein, 10.7g Fat, 111 Calories

Recipe ....

From the kicthen of ....

Serves .... Prep time .... Cook time ....

☐ Difficulty   ☐ Easy   ☐ Medium   ☐ Hard

Ingredient

....

....

....

....

....

Directions ....

....

....

....

....

....

Date: _____

MY SHOPPING LIST

Appendix A: Measurement Conversions

BASIC KITCHEN CONVERSIONS & EQUIVALENTS

DRY MEASUREMENTS CONVERSION CHART

3 TEASPOONS = 1 TABLESPOON = 1/16 CUP

6 TEASPOONS = 2 TABLESPOONS = 1/8 CUP

12 TEASPOONS = 4 TABLESPOONS = 1/4 CUP

24 TEASPOONS = 8 TABLESPOONS = 1/2 CUP

36 TEASPOONS = 12 TABLESPOONS = 3/4 CUP

48 TEASPOONS = 16 TABLESPOONS = 1 CUP

METRIC TO US COOKING CONVERSIONS

OVEN TEMPERATURES

120 °C = 250 °F

160 °C = 320 °F

180° C = 350 °F

205 °C = 400 °F

220 °C = 425 °F

LIQUID MEASUREMENTS CONVERSION CHART

8 FLUID OUNCES = 1 CUP = 1/2 PINT = 1/4 QUART

16 FLUID OUNCES = 2 CUPS = 1 PINT = 1/2 QUART

32 FLUID OUNCES = 4 CUPS = 2 PINTS = 1 QUART
 = 1/4 GALLON

128 FLUID OUNCES = 16 CUPS = 8 PINTS = 4 QUARTS = 1 GALLON

BAKING IN GRAMS

1 CUP FLOUR = 140 GRAMS

1 CUP SUGAR = 150 GRAMS

1 CUP POWDERED SUGAR = 160 GRAMS

1 CUP HEAVY CREAM = 235 GRAMS

VOLUME

1 MILLILITER = 1/5 TEASPOON

5 ML = 1 TEASPOON

15 ML = 1 TABLESPOON

240 ML = 1 CUP OR 8 FLUID OUNCES

1 LITER = 34 FL. OUNCES

US TO METRIC COOKING CONVERSIONS

1/5 TSP = 1 ML

1 TSP = 5 ML

1 TBSP = 15 ML

1 FL OUNCE = 30 ML

1 CUP = 237 ML

1 PINT (2 CUPS) = 473 ML

1 QUART (4 CUPS) = .95 LITER

1 GALLON (16 CUPS) = 3.8 LITERS

1 OZ = 28 GRAMS

1 POUND = 454 GRAMS

BUTTER

1 CUP BUTTER = 2 STICKS = 8 OUNCES = 230 GRAMS = 8 TABLESPOONS

WHAT DOES 1 CUP EQUAL

1 CUP = 8 FLUID OUNCES

1 CUP = 16 TABLESPOONS

1 CUP = 48 TEASPOONS

1 CUP = 1/2 PINT

1 CUP = 1/4 QUART

1 CUP = 1/16 GALLON

1 CUP = 240 ML

WEIGHT

1 GRAM = .035 OUNCES

100 GRAMS = 3.5 OUNCES

500 GRAMS = 1.1 POUNDS

1 KILOGRAM = 35 OUNCES

BAKING PAN CONVERSIONS

1 CUP ALL-PURPOSE FLOUR = 4.5 OZ

1 CUP ROLLED OATS = 3 OZ 1 LARGE EGG = 1.7 OZ

1 CUP BUTTER = 8 OZ 1 CUP MILK = 8 OZ

1 CUP HEAVY CREAM = 8.4 OZ

1 CUP GRANULATED SUGAR = 7.1 OZ

1 CUP PACKED BROWN SUGAR = 7.75 OZ

1 CUP VEGETABLE OIL = 7.7 OZ

1 CUP UNSIFTED POWDERED SUGAR = 4.4 OZ

BAKING PAN CONVERSIONS

9-INCH ROUND CAKE PAN = 12 CUPS

10-INCH TUBE PAN = 16 CUPS

11-INCH BUNDT PAN = 12 CUPS

9-INCH SPRINGFORM PAN = 10 CUPS

9 X 5 INCH LOAF PAN = 8 CUPS

9-INCH SQUARE PAN = 8 CUPS

Appendix B: Recipes Index

Printed in Great Britain
by Amazon

42092836R00053